Follow Your Bliss

Pop More Corks

Parables to Refresh
the Soul's Palate

Written by

David Biegemann

First Edition
Copyright © 2007
by David Biegemann

book available at
www.lulu.com

also visit
www.popmorecorks.com

ISBN: 978-0-9649345-2-8

DEDICATION

This book is dedicated to all who have passed through my doors.

David Biegemann

ACKNOWLEDGEMENTS

Thank you to my mom and dad for the emotional, spiritual, and financial support that helped me follow my passion.

For all the help I received from the professionals at Centegra Northern Illinois Medical Center, in McHenry, and Northwestern University Hospital in Chicago.

To my collaborator and editor, Richard Bencriscutto, and for special editing support, Sharon Gislason.

To everyone who helped with transportation, living arrangements, and general support during my recovery, especially, Karen Perrelli, Dean Belmonte, Theresa Schneider, and Mary Beth Gaik.

ABOUT THE AUTHOR

David Biegemann is the proprietor of Pop More Corks, a wine & cheese concession nestled on the east side of the downtown area of the popular resort destination, Lake Geneva, Wisconsin. He learned his trade during a 30-year career in the restaurant and wholesale wine business. His extensive knowledge of wine is not, however, the only thing that makes shopping for just that right bottle of wine such an engaging experience at Pop More Corks.

Some difficult life lessons have aged David's soul, like a fine mature wine. Somehow, initial discussions centering on spirits often seem to drift into other areas along with the bouquet of a Pinot Noir or Bordeaux being sampled by customers.

On the pages of *Pop More Corks* you'll be able to walk a while in David's shoes and experience the enchantment when opened wine spills over into an open soul refreshing both palate and spirit.

INTRODUCTION

David Biegemann walked the path pursued by millions of Americans seduced by stereotypical visions of success, too often represented by climbing the corporate ladder and achieving the American Dream in terms of cars, income, and a beautiful home. David was well on his way to achieving that version of fulfillment when a sudden, massive, and debilitating stroke forced him down a different Path.

Pop More Corks is the story of how one man learned to search his soul for what is truly important in life. The principles that provide people with a sense of fulfillment and happiness are not always apparent. In our culture, we often see only what the media and marketplace want us to see. David's medical crisis didn't affect his mind or his vision, but it did open his eyes to see his life in a different light.

David's rocky life path eventually led him to open his store, Pop More Corks, where every day he unlocks his door, opens a few bottles of fine wine, and the world streams in bringing so many wonderful people and their stories. To be sure, David and his customers talk wine and experience the best that the Wine Culture has to offer, but there is always much much ... more.

1

LIVING THE AMERICAN DREAM

"David, I've been thinking about what you told me earlier. I want to see you right away," Dr. Johnson, my longtime friend and trusted physician ordered after dismissing an earlier call where I described some relatively mild symptoms involving numbness in my right arm and difficulty moving my right leg.

"Well, I was hoping everything would be all right, like you said, but those symptoms, if anything are getting worse," I responded, concerned, but relieved that I would soon be under a doctor's care.

"Get down to the emergency room at All Saints and I'll meet you there right away," Dr. Johnson directed.

"I will. I should be there in about 20 minutes," I responded, aware that my wife of 16 years was off to work, but not aware of how difficult it would soon become to drive myself to the ER.

Up until that fateful day in 1997, my wife and I had been living the American Dream. I was working long hours and moving up rapidly in a major wine distribution company. My wife was a manager at the exclusive Grand Geneva complex. Her passion was anything to do with horses. My passion—well, I wasn't quite sure that mattered much. Together we acquired an estate on 12 acres including a main house, barn, fields, and horses. Although we didn't have children, to the world, it seemed we were a happy and successful couple.

The long hours began to take a toll on our relationship. With little time for each other, our marriage began to falter. What seemed so important at the time, chasing after success in material terms, proved to be an illusion. The signs were there, but it was impossible to change course. The choices we make in life are based on our values. Divorce can never be good, can it? The truth—our marriage suffered from the beginning.

My preoccupation with work and her consuming interest in horses hid the fundamental problem—we never established a mutually loving and caring relationship. Had we both been more in touch with our inner selves, our souls, I believe a higher quality relationship may have evolved. The fundamental goal of our journey through life is to develop our inner central spiritual core.

Though we both had unmet spiritual needs during our marriage, we weren't aware this was even a problem. We had been seduced to climb on to the relentless treadmill in pursuit of material success. Once on, getting off would not be easy. Navigating the demands of each workday, paying the bills and maintaining our property, left little time or energy to worry about anything else.

For fifteen years we both worked without feeling a sense of acting with any purpose beyond earning an income. For fifteen years we remained married with little love left in the relationship. Without warning fate would intervene, changing everything.

During a regular checkup I was told that unless I changed my current life style routines and began to do things much differently, there could be serious medical complications down the road. Medical issues were nothing new to me. I'd lived with and responsibly managed diabetes and high blood pressure for years. Taking the doctor's warning seriously, I shared these concerns with my wife.

"I know how much you love our home and grounds here, but I just left my doctor and he told me in no uncertain terms that unless I cut back, the stress could kill me," I opened, believing what I was saying.

"Just what are you suggesting?" was her stunned response.

"This place—it's more than I can handle. I'm working three jobs, long hours, and when I get home there's always so much to do around here. I never get a chance to rest. I'm afraid we need to sell this place," I declared.

"What are you talking about? We've been getting along here for years and now you're suggesting we give it all up? Over my dead body!" she cried, expressing no sympathy, empathy, or concern for what I was dealing with.

I was not surprised by her reaction, but I was also not ready to force any significant changes. Instead I simply gave up on our marriage and soon found myself in an affair with someone who was sympathetic, empathetic, and concerned about my needs. Months went by during which my wife and I continued to pass the days as before—living together, yet alone. Little did we know a medical time bomb ticking away inside my head would soon end our emotional stalemate.

Unknown to me, a genetic predisposition led to a malformation in a cluster of blood vessels in my brain. This type of disorder typically results in a medical crisis sometime during middle age. Unaware of what was about to happen, but possibly sensing change was coming, on my own I ended the affair and began a period dedicated to rebuilding my marriage. Then, one day my wife and I stopped for lunch after running some morning errands, including another routine doctor's visit where I was told everything was great.

While sitting at the table, I experienced a strange warm surging sensation streaming deep from within my head and chest.

Realizing something was very wrong, I said to my wife, "Oh my God, I think I may have just had a stroke."

There was no pain associated with what had happened, so I decided to get up to see if I was all right. It felt like there was a big wad of gum stuck to the bottom of my right shoe when I tried to walk away from the table. There was a certain weakness in my right leg and a decided lack of balance. Not noticing any other symptoms, I sat back down and finished my meal, hoping the symptoms were temporary.

"I'm really not feeling all that well. Why don't you drive home," I requested.

"Certainly, let's get going," my wife responded.

Once home, I tested my leg again, it was still sluggish, but I was able to walk at that point. Knowing something was not right, but not realizing the seriousness of what was unfolding inside my brain, I called to consult with my doctor.

"During lunch I felt an unusual warm flushing sensation and afterwards it became difficult for me to move my right leg," I opened.

"David, I just saw you. You passed every test. Don't worry about it," was his hurried, overly optimistic response.

"OK, if you say so. Anyway, I hope you're right," I said, in some denial about what might be happening and wanting to believe my doctor.

My wife had left for work when a few minutes later my doctor called back and reversed his earlier position; he requested that I meet him at the hospital.

While paused at a stoplight on my way to the hospital, my right side completely shut down. Luckily I had recently purchased a cell phone and a 911 call soon had me riding to the emergency room in an ambulance. The delay in treatment actually proved to be providential.

Had I been diagnosed and treated earlier with the standard clot-busting drugs, the bleeding in my brain would have been more severe and could have been fatal. Later tests would find the bleed and the next day doctors induced a coma to slow the swelling. Surgery relieved the building pressure and I went to intensive care. My prognosis was not good.

2

OPENING DOORS TO LET THE UNIVERSE IN

As I open this door, may I be open to all that the Universe may bring to me. I ask to be receptive to whatever and whoever comes my way this glorious day.

These thoughts have become a regular morning mantra as I prepare for each new day of life, and each new day as the proprietor of Pop More Corks by turning the key opening the front door.

Have you ever felt that you were in exactly the right place at exactly the right time, doing exactly what you were meant to do? Despite everything that had happened to me medically, I'd been feeling just that way for the first time in my life.

On one memorable day three women walked through the Pop More Cork doors arm in arm—one in her 50's, Marika, another in her 60's, Jessica, and a more elderly grand dame, Lorene, in her 70's.

"Welcome to Pop More Corks! What brings you ladies to Lake Geneva today?" I opened.

"We saw your wine tasting sign and decided this was something we should check out," Marika offered as an explanation, speaking for the group.

The deeper truth was more personal. Lorene had been struggling with health problems and had been living in a nursing home until Marika began taking care of her, allowing Lorene to progress toward a much higher quality of life back in her home.

It had been months since any of them had been out to just relax and unwind. This was the weekend dedicated to refreshing their spirits.

The wine tasting began with a fine, but reasonably priced Spanish Verdeho and continued on to several other unique white wines.

"This Verdeho is crisp and clean and refreshing and comes from a winery in the Rueda district of Spain. On a hot summer

August day this is a perfect wine to quench your thirst," I began.

"I don't think I've ever had a wine like this before," was Jessica's enthusiastic response to her first sip.

During the course of conducting a wine tasting, besides describing the wines, I always try to learn more about the precious souls that wander into my day.

"So, what is it you do for a living?" I directed at Marika.

"Oh, I take care of her," pointing at Lorene. I also love to throw pots—Raku pottery," she added.

I listened intently as Marika described what made the Raku technique so appealing. The process involves a more free-flow color result from the glazing. Marika's face beamed as she talked passionately about her creative outlet.

"Look, her eyes are even closed. It's like she's praying when she talks about her pottery," Jessica pointed out, teasing, but in awe and respectful of her friend's love for crafting in clay.

"I can see that," I responded.

"So, Marika, you said you take care of Lorene. What did you mean by that?" I continued.

"Well, I'm there for her every day to make sure she has the help she needs to manage life's normal daily routines," Marika explained.

"You know what, I think you just enjoy being with her, and taking care of her is just your excuse," I announced confidently, having sensed that their relationship was deeper and based on mutual love and respect.

"You're absolutely right! Lorene is my father's wife. When she developed a series of illnesses that made it difficult for her to get around and take care of herself, my heart went out to her. I'd been visiting her in the nursing home and decided she could be doing much better. It took some time, but as you can see, she's up and around now and back living in the home she shared with my father."

"I can't believe Lorene ever had problems with her mobility, she looks so fit and vital now," I commented, looking at Lorene as she blushed in response to my compliment.

"Lorene is a very special and talented lady. She has performed in musical theater and opera in Chicago during a long and successful career. Music and the arts have always been in her blood," Marika went on.

I had some Sarah Brightman playing in the background. I noticed Lorene responding to this unique brand of opera for popular consumption.

"You seem to be enjoying the music. Do you recognize the artist?" I asked, directing my question to Lorene.

"I just love Sarah's performances. She sets a high standard of artistic excellence, one, I'm afraid, I aspired to, but never quite reached. You know, I believe in God, but in the past, when I've been asked what my religion is, to my surprise the first answer that comes to mind is that my religion is music. Music has always been the inspiration that keeps my soul alive," Lorene shared with the group as she took a sip of a rich, lush, complex Santa Barbara Chardonnay.

"I share your admiration for Sarah as an artist, but the real reason I've added her to my collection of background CD's is because her music reminds me of my mother," I reported, feeling comfortable opening up some of my private thoughts.

"Why is that," Lorene asked.

"Before my mother passed, she was suffering from the effects of several strokes and was barely able to communicate. Although our conversations were limited, I hoped she might still be able to appreciate music the way she used to, so I got her a CD player and one of the CD's I put on for her was this one from Sarah Brightman. Listening to Sarah always brought a big smile to her face, a clear sign of delight and recognition, deeply contrasting her typical condition struggling with pain and discomfort," I added. My words and the music, emotionally returning me to my mother's bedside, caused a sudden and unexpected welling up of tears in my eyes.

All three women were moved by this unashamed display of raw emotion from a man they barely knew.

"I can see you must have really loved your mother and I respect the fact that you are able to express such emotions," Jessica added, hoping to validate my feelings.

"She meant the world to me. The three of you don't know how much I appreciate being able to share this with you. So, what about you? I know something about your two friends. How about you," I inquired, brushing the last tears from my cheeks.

"Well, I've worked with children all my life. I began with preschool students, then after a long career spent my last years teaching computer science to middle school kids, before retiring last year," Jessica shared, also beaming with pride in a professional life full of a sense of accomplishment and service while making a difference in the lives of thousands of children during her tenure.

The wine tasting lasted about an hour, and yet no one was aware of the clock ticking. They'd slipped into a timeless zone where the sharing led to a communion of souls, each validating and supporting the other's dignity and worth.

As proof of the significance of their brief time together, the next day the ladies returned, cameras in hand, wanting to revisit and document their warm experience at Pop More Corks—hugs and kisses mandatory as they left the store and Lake Geneva to return to their homes stronger, healthier, happier individuals, and closer as friends.

*P*arable *R*eflections

My early morning intention to be open to whatever opportunity for growth and sharing the Universe of possibilities might bring my way was certainly realized. I benefited as much as the three angelic souls who were brought to me that day by the mysterious process of Synchronicity.

Our intentions, our prayers, are somehow registered for processing on a spiritual network connecting us. Like some kind of spiritual email system, those intentions, concerns, needs, requests, shared by individuals, bring about opportunities for what seem like coincidental encounters, but they are not random events. They bring together people who can make a difference in the lives of those they meet because they share a common intention.

The phenomenon of Synchronicity is mysterious and magical, but a real and vital force in our lives if we only Believe and open up to its potential. One of our greatest gifts is Free Will—our ability to create our own destiny for good or ill.

Each and every day we can exercise our choice to attract good, positive things, events, and people into our lives, or the opposite, by dwelling on the negative. If we are open, and our intentions are true, good will be drawn to us.

We can learn so much from each other, but only if we are open to share and give. We are here to grow spiritually. Set your intentions and take a spiritual step forward each and every day.

Joseph Campbell, author of, *The Power of Myth,* describes a conference of Catholic priests and Buddhist monks probing the similarities among the world's great religions.

"Would you please try and encapsulate your religious theology?" an open-minded Catholic priest asked of a Buddhist monk.

Appearing puzzled at first, but after a moment of reflection he replied, "I don't think we have a theology . . . I think we dance!"

Like Lorene's honest declaration that music was her religion, the purpose of any true religion is to enrich the soul's vitality, to encourage our creative impulses as a mechanism to grow spiritually and reach out to others.

On the day of their second visit, before leaving, Lorene reached over the counter, took my hand, and gave me a kiss.

While holding her hand, I said, "Thank you, and by the way, I like your religion!"

As the Pop More Corks clock reached 7:00 PM, once again it was time to close and lock the doors. Key in hand, I thought my evening mantra.

As I close this door, I am thankful for all the wonderful people and experiences that have been brought to me this day.

3

FAITH, BELIEF, AND COMMITMENT

Several days passed while I was in an induced coma waiting for my doctors to determine that it was safe for me to regain consciousness. My AVM (Arterial Vascular Malformation) first ruptured, causing my stroke, before natural healing and clotting mechanisms managed to stop the bleed.

Normally, major arteries branch into smaller ones, then capillaries, then small veins, to larger veins. In my case, there was a region in my brain where a major artery fed directly into a major vein with no small vessels in between. When someone is born with this kind of AVM, there will usually be some related medical crisis during middle age.

I was fortunate to survive the AVM incident. Many do not. Secondly, the effects of the stroke could have been much more debilitating. Being born with an AVM is not, as far as is known, hereditary. Other than a memory of passing out for no apparent reason during football practice once in high school, I can't think of any possibly related symptoms. That is also typical. If passing out was related to my AVM, it may have been a blessing it wasn't discovered at that time.

Any medical intervention 25 years ago would have been much less sophisticated and therefore, potentially much more dangerous than what vascular surgeons can do today to repair an AVM.

The cause of a typical stroke is a blood-blocking clot. In that case, brain cells begin to die from lack of oxygen. When an AVM bleeds out, brain cells drown in the blood that surrounds them. In both cases, once dead, brain cells do not regenerate. The way people recover from any stroke is to rewire the brain's pathways.

Based on electrical impulses, the healing that can happen is for the patient, through physical therapy, to route new paths for the signals to reach the areas cut off by the stroke. Before therapy could begin, first my surgeons had to save my life by relieving the pressure building up as a result of the bleed.

Part of this phase was inducing a coma to reduce my blood pressure and heart rate. The surgeons created an opening near the bleed to relieve the pressure. Five days of intensive care were needed for my condition to stabilize. Out of intensive care, I was moved to a hospital bed for three more days. It would be months until my doctors determined what specifically had caused my stroke.

Medical imaging was not able to generate clear pictures because of the blood pool. Eventually, the AVM was identifed. Regardless of the cause, standard stroke rehabilitation would be ordered as my treatment. Before physical therapy could begin, I had to be brought back to consciousness. The drugs used to keep me in the coma were slowly withdrawn while my doctors waited for me to wake up.

"David, you're back with us! How do you feel?" my neurosurgeon asked.

"A little groggy, but I'm not in any pain," I managed to get out with a weak voice.

"Can you help me with some tests? Would that be all right?" he patiently suggested.

"I'll do my best," I responded.

"Try to move your right foot," he asked.

"I'm trying right now. Is anything happening?" I wondered, because I couldn't feel much along my leg.

"I'm touching your foot right now. Can you feel that?" the doctor asked.

"Yes, I sure can," I confidently answered.

The doctor continued with various needles probing all along my right side. Although I couldn't move my right arm or leg, there was then, and always has been, feeling on my right side. There were other, more friendly and recognizable faces surrounding my bed that day.

My parents were there along with my wife, her mother and siblings, and my brother. Unlike near-death accounts where a person may experience the recognizable images of dear departed loved ones, it was a good sign that everyone I saw around me was still living.

Before the surgery, I asked the doctors if my condition was serious enough to inform my family. They advised that I contact them. Teresa, my wife, called everyone to the hospital.

I knew I wasn't dead, but seeing my family, realized I'd survived a very close and real brush with death. It was both comforting and terrifying to have them all there.

With the medical crisis over, it was imperative that my physical therapy begin as soon as possible. I was discharged from the main hospital and signed into the rehabilitation ward for stroke patients.

Soon after my stay in intensive care was over my parents left to go back home to Texas. They weren't in a position to provide me with ongoing support. During the next several months, Teresa was there for me during the initial phases of my rehabilitation.

Knowing my rehabilitation was going to take months, and understanding that the recovery process would require 100% of my effort and focus, I felt the need to settle the issue of whether or not my marriage was going to survive. When the question was put to her, after a couple of days of contemplation, Teresa had to honestly admit that it was time to move on.

At that point I realized there would only be one person responsible for my recovery, and that was ME!

Although my wife was initially supportive, and although we were making an effort to improve our marriage, the relationship remained devoid of any real emotional union. During my brief affair, those needs for passion, empathy, communication, and sensitivity, were met, but instead of moving away from my marriage when my wife filed for divorce, about a year before the stroke, I felt compelled to try one more time to save my marriage. At that point, powerful childhood scripts took over.

I had seen my parents go through difficult periods in their marriage as I was growing up.

I overheard a number of heated arguments when threats were made, but the fundamental principle, to work out problems and stay married for the sake of the family, kept my parents together. Over the years I saw the good and bad in their marriage and concluded that the good outweighed the bad, making preserving the marriage worthwhile. Now it was my turn to apply this ingrained principle in my life.

Through some harsh self evaluation, I blamed myself for much of what was wrong in my own marriage and concluded that, rededicated to my wife, our relationship could thrive. Unfortunately, family finances worsened and we did have to sell our estate and move into a much smaller home. I was several months into this phase of marital reconstruction when the stroke hit.

Sensing intuitively that I had to devote all my energy and what inspiration and vitality I had left to my recovery, I didn't try to hold the marriage together. My intuition proved to be very accurate. When rehabilitation began, it consumed me. I was forced to rely on myself to accomplish my goal of achieving total recovery. Although full recovery is always the hope, there are many forms of complete recovery that don't involve the restoration of pre-stroke physical functions.

I came to perceive Teresa's decision to move on without me as a blessing because I was forced to rely on myself and my inner strength to rebuild my life and physical function. Yes, my team of doctors, therapists, and friends would be there for support, but without my complete dedication, belief, and faith in the process, not nearly as much would have been accomplished. In a spiritual sense, this was a period of being reborn.

The fundamental spiritual principles we associate with Biblical Christianity, the need for Faith and Belief, translate as core aspects of a healthy soul, no matter what religion one practices—no matter if one accepts a Higher Power or not. Joseph Campbell in his book, *The Hero with a Thousand Faces*, describes the journey everyone must take to nurture the refinement of the soul. This was the time when I began my hero's struggle—a period rebuilding the foundations of my soul.

Every day we make decisions and choices that affect the outcome of our lives. Once an important decision or choice is made, it is imperative that you believe 100% in the direction you've chosen in order to realize the full potential of that choice. Belief and Faith go hand in hand. Belief keeps you on track and Faith provides the ongoing hope that everything will work out for the best in time.

I sensed I would have to take full responsibility for my decisions and the rehabilitation process, then, according to the principle of Detachment, give all up to a Higher Power, the Universe, and accept what comes. In another blessing from believing in these principles, I don't remember being depressed or angry over becoming the victim of a stroke and the result it had on my life.

I chose only to focus on the recovery process, day by day, moment by present moment, not worried about what I couldn't do anymore, but completely focusing on what I could accomplish. The message carried in the Serenity Prayer, "God grant me the Serenity to accept the things I cannot change, the Courage to change the things I can, and the Wisdom to know the difference," exemplifies a spiritual principle that has helped countless people who struggle with tragedy, illness, addiction, and depression. I was spiritually prepared to begin therapy.

My physical therapist was trained to work on leg function and my occupational therapist worked on movement in my arm, while my speech therapist worked on cognitive issues. On the first day of therapy, my leg was tested.

"David, let me help you. You're going to first sit up, then, I'll take you over to the wall," Thomas began.

Our initial work together involved assessing just how much, if any, weight I could put on my right leg. Assisted to stand up against the wall, I was asked to begin to lean on the affected leg. The leg immediately gave way. Various kinds of physical therapy continued over weeks and months producing small, but noticeable improvements.

Thomas was right there to keep me from falling over. During the first several weeks I relearned how to get out of bed, into a wheelchair, and use the restroom—the basics of beginning to rely on myself for my daily needs. I benefited from my physical therapist's unyielding belief in my ability to make progress and improve. Among the successful techniques used were electrical and cold stimulation.

Initially, I was completely wheelchair bound. I couldn't use a walker because that required two working hands and arms. After slow, painful progress gaining strength and some movement in my leg, I progressed to walking with a cane.

The physical therapists worked primarily with my leg function. The daily repetitive exercises were grueling. Little by little I was first able to lift my leg off the bed just slightly, then a little more, and a little more. When enough progress had been made, the next phase was to stand next to my bed.

A cane at first substituted for my right leg, then, slowly, small amounts of body weight were transferred to that leg until I was ready to take my first steps assisted by a cane. Small first steps led to walks around the ward, then throughout the complex, simulating the ambulatory challenges I would face when released from the hospital. A right leg brace provides just enough stability and ankle support to make walking a once-again reliable way to get around. All of this rehabilitation took time and money, most of which was provided by insurance.

Keep in mind, your insurance company is looking for regular signs of improvement. This may not seem fair, but if two or three weeks go by and no progress is noted by your team of doctors, at that point your insurance company will be making plans to stop funding your therapy.

Based on the type of injury, illness, or stroke you may have suffered, there are clear expectations for your recovery. Never let a doctor, or therapist, or anyone involved with your case, set a limit to the improvement you can make. They can't possibly factor in your will, and the will of your Creator.

Regarding my arm and hand function, I am certain that were I to dedicate a long-term intensive therapy effort to improving my current function, I would see definite improvement. I made a clear choice to move back into the day-to-day world rather than stay in therapy until all possible progress was achieved.

I spent three months living in the rehabilitation ward before being discharged as an outpatient. My wife's sister provided a residence near the rehab center and transitional support while I was learning to walk and drive again. Within three months I was back at my old job two days a week.

Because of several epileptic seizures, not uncommon aftereffects of any brain trauma, I wasn't allowed to drive until a certain amount of time had passed seizure free. I also had to practice driving with one hand and one leg until I could drive confidently on my own. Before my stroke I'd worked for a wine and liquor distributor, Judge & Dolph Inc., owned by Bill Wirtz.

Mr. Wirtz was also the owner of the Chicago Black Hawks Hockey Team as well as other business interests. Although wealthy, Mr. Wirtz was known for being, let's say, an efficient money manager. After working only two years for the company, ten months passed from the time of my debilitating stroke to the day I returned to work part time. For that entire period, a good friend from work found me either at the hospital or at home and handed me my normal paycheck to support my rehabilitation. Bill Wirtz and the company believed in me, and that helped me believe in my ability to eventually return to work.

Most people in situations like mine find their the position terminated. Filing for disability would be next. That would normally mean losing your health insurance and the coverage that's paying for rehabilitation. Fortunately for me, Judge & Dolph was compassionate and loyal.

The goal of rehab is to help the patient recover as much normal function as possible, not always including being able to resume prior employment. It is often a slow, painful process. One important component of the process is to structure the patient's day.

First of all, it's up at six in the morning, seven days a week. Only Sunday afternoon was free of therapy. The patients can't wear hospital gowns at therapy sessions. That meant I had to learn how to dress myself with my one useful hand and leg. Typically, I wore sweat pants, a T-shirt, socks and shoes. Try tying your shoes with one hand. Then, it was down three floors to the rehabilitation center.

A series of 45-minute sessions filled my day, including physical, occupational, speech, and cognitive therapies. Pool work was especially encouraging as buoyant forces supported the efforts of my weak limbs. Outside the pool there was no substitute for repeated efforts to lift my arm just a little bit higher, or move my leg just a little bit farther during each session.

Early on I also had to learn how to negotiate three meals a day. Developing new skills for using utensils with one hand required adjustments. Initially, I was confined to a wheelchair.

The patient residence was on one floor, organized with rooms to the outside and a central commons where meals and meetings were held. An interesting architectural feature of the common room was that the tables were suspended on cables from the ceiling so that wheelchairs could easily roll under them.

At any one time, there was a mix of patients struggling to recover function from strokes, from falls, from accidents and injuries. They came and went without necessarily forming supportive relationships with one another, primarily because their days were so filled with sessions and goals to accomplish that there was little time or energy left at the end of a day for casual socializing. One common activity, the simple game Yahtzee, turned into a cognitive therapy challenge for me.

My brother-in-law brought me a handheld version of the game I could play by myself, knowing I'd enjoyed playing for many years. After rolling the dice, and looking at the numbers on each die, I had no idea how to interpret what I was seeing for scoring purposes.

I was aware I'd played the game many times growing up and even recently before the stroke. When I also realized the stroke left me with this relatively subtle cognitive issue, I made a commitment to relearn the game. There were other difficulties. I couldn't remember common codes, telephone numbers, and passwords anymore. They would all have to be imbedded all over again in my memory. These were some of the cognitive side effects from the stroke that were not uncovered by my team of therapists.

This is an example of how any patient can become one's own therapist by adopting the attitude of taking responsibility for one's total wellness, and not just leaving every decision in the hands of the professionals. Hours and hours of playing and replaying Yahtzee gradually carved new pathways in my brain. Again, to help with my cognitive reprogramming, I asked for my laptop computer.

It took special permission, but my regular therapy soon involved computer-based activities. The relatively minor cognitive issues cleared up in short order, while the physical problems improved slowly over time. Many of the other stroke patients on the ward were struggling with serious cognitive deterioration. I was constantly reminded of how fortunate I was to be dealing primarily with movement difficulties as opposed to mental function setbacks.

Before being discharged from the rehabilitation unit, I had to overcome a number of medical setbacks. Because I was spending most of my time flat on my back in bed, there was a risk of blood clots developing. When my doctors noticed swelling in my legs, it became apparent that clots were responsible. Blood clots are potentially life threatening, if left untreated. They can break loose and make their way to critical vessels in the brain or heart or lungs with catastrophic results.

A team of specialists was assigned to my case. Each had a different perspective regarding the basic cause of my condition and the best course of treatment. Although they should have been consulting with each other regularly and arriving at a consensus, that is not always what happens in the rush of a doctor's hectic daily schedule.

Because of the clots, I was readmitted to the hospital ward. It was Thanksgiving weekend and my neurosurgeon was out of town. I woke up one evening as I was being prepped for an injection.

"Nurse, I wasn't aware that any treatment for my clots had been ordered. What is in the shot you're planning to give me?" I questioned, groggy, but concerned enough to act as my own patient advocate.

"This is a blood thinner that should break up the clots in your legs," the nurse answered, acting on an order by my vascular specialist. He hadn't consulted with my neurologist to learn that my stroke was caused by a bleed that my body had stopped through a clotting process. The blood thinners would have almost certainly triggered the bleed in my brain to resume, this time with potentially life-threatening results.

Thinking clearly enough to be engaged in what was happening, I declared, "You're not giving me that shot until my neurosurgeon gets back to say it's OK!"

The nurse respected my position and did not administer the blood thinners. I took it upon myself to make a life-or-death medical decision using my own good common sense. There were risks.

The clots in my legs could break loose and cause more severe problems elsewhere. On the other hand, the massive dose of blood thinner may have dissolved the clots in my legs and the clot in my brain that was keeping me alive. When the neurosurgeon returned, my refusal to cooperate was validated. I learned that the shot very likely could have killed me.

Seldom does a person have the opportunity to adequately prepare to become one's own patient advocate when a medical emergency strikes. Doctors are only human and often overworked. Statistics show that many patients suffer as a result of a wrong prescription or a mishandled medical procedure. It is important that every patient learn as much as one can, ask questions, and respond to gut instincts when being treated. Don't be afraid to take a stand when you feel it is the right thing to do.

An alternative procedure was used to solve my clot problem. Entering through my neck, a catheter was snaked through a vein to the point between the clot in my leg and my heart. There, a wire mesh screen with hooks on it was deployed. Rushing blood set the screen in front of the clot. If the clot did break loose, it would get caught in the screen. No blood thinners were needed.

Patients typically believe in and trust their doctors to make every medical decision regarding their case and the best course of action. Doctors often have the training, equipment, and medications to deliver modern medical miracles to patients suffering from serious diseases or trauma. Nevertheless, it is always important for patients to understand as much as possible about what's causing their problem and what the options for treatment are.

At that point, the patient must take personal responsibility for what will take place, believe in the course of action that is chosen, and realize that it is the patient's responsibility to become well, not the doctor's. Wellness is a complex mind-body-spirit phenomenon.

A pill or a surgery will rarely, alone, result in a restored sense of Purpose and a desire to return to a place of being able to function in their former day-to-day world. Too often, being ill can become a crutch, an excuse, to give up on the struggle we all face everyday to get up and make a productive contribution to the world we live in, to make the most of the gifts and function we do have at our disposal, regardless of how an illness or accident has impacted us.

Where there is life, and a clear mind, there is the potential for the spark of the Divine within each of us to build into a flame of inspiration for ourself and others. After my stroke and after being discharged from the hospital, I found myself in a new relationship with a mother and her two children.

While we were exploring our relationship's potential, she took her children on a trip where they were physically very active. Mother and children went biking, waded out to an island to hunt clams, pitched tents, and hiked long trails. Upon her return, and although she appreciated many of the things I brought to her family, especially my perspective on the world beyond what we can see, touch, and measure, she wasn't sure my qualities were enough to outweigh the issue of my physical limitations. Her hesitation over this often triggered spirited debates.

"I may not be able to hike down the canyon walls, but I would love to take you and your children to the Grand Canyon and have you stand on the rim and experience the mystery and magic of that panorama," I suggested.

"David, it is only rock carved out by rushing water over millions of years . . . nothing mysterious about it," was her testy comeback.

"Have you ever been there? You've got to go sometime, because it's definitely more than that," I pressed, knowing I was right because I'd been there and had been powerfully moved.

"Well, we'll see . . . possibly some day we can all go," she responded without attacking my position further.

*P*arable *R*eflections

There is a place for what science can prove and there is a place for what we can know through our senses, but what science can't explain is the wonder in the universe. You can't stand on the edge of the Grand Canyon without knowing, without a doubt, that there is something more than the rocks and river and trees—someone, some power greater than anything we could possibly know, that exists. It is a profound feeling that sinks right down to the depths of your heart and soul.

Although I regretted walking away from a good relationship because of the effects of my stroke, this experience made it clear that my new understanding and awareness of the importance of the spiritual dimension made any sacrifices on the physical plane worthwhile. I remember beginning to share my new insights with others. Around this time, the profound concept of the unity of all things, living and non-living, became even more clear to me.

I was just an average guy from Mundelein, Illinois, but somehow, someway, something was connecting me to a pebble at the bottom of the Yangtze River in China in such a way that we were influencing each other. That thought led to the realization that there was a much greater power than I had any understanding of, responsible for that connection. It also seemed appropriate that this being was even beyond having a name.

Thanks in large measure to my physical therapist who could see my potential to progress out of my wheelchair, and never let me believe otherwise, at the end of my three month stay in rehab, I walked out of the hospital, trusty cane in hand, in a position to reclaim my life as a productive member of society.

Medical science made an important contribution to my wellness, but my willingness to allow a greater power to work through my own belief and faith that I would heal, made as great a contribution.

4

"NOW I KNOW WHY WE CAME HERE"

As I open this door, may I be open to allowing all possibilities to be brought to me. I ask to be receptive to whatever and whoever comes my way this glorious day.

After being open for several months, I began to notice that so many people who walked through my Pop More Corks doors were carrying the burden of some health issue. These people were often open to sharing some intimate details of their struggle. When these kinds of conversations surfaced, I would pass on messages to focus on what you can do as opposed to being despondent over the functions you've lost. One day a family walked in.

A husband, his wife, the man's brother and sister-in-law were engaged in the lively exchange of a wine tasting session.

"I have a unique selection of wines chosen from small producers all over the world," I began.

"And why is that?" the husband asked.

"Small producers make wines that exhibit characteristics based on the type of grapes used and expressing the terroir in which they are grown," I explained.

"I'm not sure what you mean?"

"Put simply, each of the wines I've selected for my store offers unique flavors. Too often the large wineries produce a production line product without much character. In an effort to make wines that appeal to a broad range of palates, large producers will formulate a technically correct wine that lacks character and through marketing create an unjustified reputation and exorbitant price," was my answer based on years of experience, study, and knowledge of the worldwide wine trade.

"That's a perspective I hadn't considered," the husband responded, clearly interested and somewhat knowledgeable about wines.

His wife was not at all drawn to the unfolding wine culture experience. Standing off to the side, she refused an offer to taste some wine. During the course of the wine tasting, I noticed the husband clearly limping as he moved about the store.

"I can see you're having some difficulty walking. What are you dealing with?" I inquired, fully empathetic as I was recovering from a recent hip replacement.

"I'm afraid I'm on the other side of some serious knee surgery and I'm not healing up the way I'd hoped," he shared.

"I know how you feel. I've just had hip surgery and I wish I could say my artificial hip was any where as good as the original," I shared.

"This is the worst setback I've ever experienced. I've always been a competitive runner. I can't even jog now, and I'm so worried I may never recover to where I was before my injury," the husband added, clearly upset and now getting emotional.

"It's a tough situation you're in, but no reason to give up. Dig into your rehab and give it everything you've got. If you're meant to regain your running ability, it will happen," I offered, yes, words of encouragement, but based on the personal experience of rehabbing out of the wheelchair after my stroke.

"I'd like to believe you're right, but at the moment, things don't look good," he said, finding it difficult to overcome the despondency of his current state of disability.

"Maybe someone is trying to tell you something. When one door closes, another can open and be just the right portal to put you on the best possible Path for your life," I continued, again having walked in the runner's shoes.

"I hear what you're saying, but without running, I feel like half a man," he added.

"Running is great and if you can get back to running again, that will be great, but it is possible for you to find happiness another way, because, you know what, you might not be able to run again, then, what are you going to do," I shared honestly.

During the entire wine tasting session and through all the conversations about wine and these other matters, the man's wife, although not directly involved, had been listening. The wine tasting over, some wine purchased, money in the till, they paused at the counter.

"You're going to be OK . . . whatever is supposed to happen will happen," I shared as the man walked toward the front door.

His wife remained at the counter waiting until her husband was outside.

"Now I know why we came here today," she said with gratitude to me before leaving the shop to join her husband.

The powerful principle of synchronicity once again brought people together who were in a position to help each other. Through being open and willing to share, perspective, empathy, and wisdom turned defeat into victory.

More and more I was constantly asking myself why the people who walked through my Pop More Corks doors were brought there. Day after day it became clear it was never only about wine.

*P*arable *R*eflections

Every day we all have powerful opportunities to make a difference in the lives of others. The things we say, the things we do, can nudge others forward. Recognizing this responsibility can seem a daunting challenge until you realize that everyone is in the same position.

A Pop More Corks wine tasting experience begins with a small, simple, but always potent act of giving. Any act of giving will trigger a giving response. Through this simple spiritual mechanism, people can be uplifted toward support and sharing instead of competition and exploitation. Remember, though, for this transaction of giving to be completed, an offer has to be accepted.

Today, faced with the world's daunting global problems of climate change, hunger, illness, and economic deprivation, it is difficult to believe that any one person can make a difference. We are all spiritually programmed to seek a sense that we can be a force for Good. Know that through one human interaction at a time, one good deed at a time, one compliment at a time, you can be a formidable force for positive change.

Through conversations with customers, I am learning that everyone has unique gifts to offer the world. Our trials and tribulations, no matter how difficult, can offer an opportunity to inspire someone else to be able to fight through their own problems.

As the Pop More Corks clock reached 7:00 PM, once again it was time to close and lock the doors. Key in hand, I thought my evening mantra.

As I close this door, I am thankful for all the wonderful people and experiences that have been brought to me this day.

5

WHAT IS IT YOU HAVE TO OFFER?

When people lose physical abilities as a result of an illness or accident, they often dwell on what they can no longer do, instead of recognizing that they still have choices. A runner who can no longer run, a baseball player who can no longer throw a ball, an artist who can no longer hold a brush, what choices do they still have?

I suffered a massive stroke that cost me the use of my right side, and yet looking back, I believe this to be a Blessing. Yes, there are physical things I no longer can do, but the stroke forced me to recognize that there were other, possibly more important gifts I had to offer the world I now lived in as a disabled person.

After three months of intensive rehabilitation, I walked out of the rehabilitation ward and back to my old job in wine sales. At first, just two days a week, then full time resuming my position as district manager which transitioned to a new role as a key account manager. I was now calling on the exclusive high-end restaurant accounts where my way with people and my knowledge of the finer points of wine and how to integrate the wine culture into a business were invaluable to building up that kind of sophisticated account. One of my regular stops was a well known, well respected restaurant in Geneva, Illinois, named 302 West.

I'd known the owners, a husband and wife, for several years. With a comfortable, well established personal and professional relationship, I looked forward to my time talking wine with the owner and sharing stories with a good friend. One of the issues with servicing this particular restaurant was a formidable flight of stairs leading up to the bar where the owner conducted all wine business.

On the first day visiting Joel after my stroke, I did not hesitate to fight my way up those stairs. Joel could see that his old friend was struggling with the aftereffects of a stroke.

"David, look, it's no problem, from now on I'll meet you downstairs. Just let me know when you arrive and I'll come down to meet you," Joel suggested, caring about my difficulties and valuing our relationship enough to make adjustments on my behalf.

"No, that's not necessary. It's something I'm able to do. Yes, it takes me a little bit longer, but it's good for me," I didn't hesitate to say.

Of course there were many other adjustments I had to make to continue servicing my customers. I organized a special carrying bag so that I didn't have to use two hands to bring the wine samples to my customers. Most of the activities I used to take for granted, I could still carry out, I just had to plan more, take my time, and often figure out ways around getting the task done with one fully functioning hand and leg.

Joel was knowledgeable about wine, had an excellent palate, and chose wonderful wines to compliment the fresh seasonal food on his menu. There wasn't much for me to teach Joel about wine, so our wine tasting sessions were more about sharing and supporting each other on this subject we were both passionate about. As the weeks went by, I began to notice there were more and more days when I stopped in for a sales session and Joel wasn't in the restaurant.

More worrisome, on many of the days when he was there, Joel declined to taste the wines I brought for him to experience. When we had a normal tasting session, he would often leave the room for a while, before returning. Joel was dealing with some sort of problem. After one session, our conversation drifted away from wine.

"David, we've been friends for years. I knew you before your stroke. I can see you're struggling with the aftermath, but how have you managed to go on after such a personal disaster?" Joel asked, digressing into a rare personal area.

"I won't pretend that it hasn't been difficult, but it's taught me a lot about myself. I know what I can do despite my disability, but more, I've learned about what I still have to offer in spite of my physical handicap."

"I can really see what you mean. When we're together I don't feel like you have a disability at all, and it's because of your attitude," Joel said, passing on a compliment to an old, valued friend.

"Many in my position have to fight through the devastating feeling that their choices have been ripped from their control," I replied.

"Was that a problem for you?" Joel asked.

"Yes it was, early on, but I soon learned that no matter what circumstances you find yourself in after a tragedy, we all always have one basic choice still in our control and that is how we react and respond to those circumstances," I shared, still working out the details of this perspective in my own mind.

At the end of a conversation, people often say, "Have a good day," suggesting that this affirmation is a choice and not necessarily up to chance.

That important primary choice we all have is to either focus on the negative—what you can't do, or refocus on the positive—what you can do and what you still have to offer. Each day, no matter what life brings, we always have that choice to make which will shape our lives in a dramatic fashion for good or ill.

In the summer of 2003 edition of, *Parabola,* the theme of *imprisonment* is reviewed. People can be imprisoned by bars of iron, or by expectations, or fears, such as the inability to control the passage of time, or the fear of losing something valued like possessions, power, one's health, or a physical function. Inner prisons, their bars formed by psychological distress, can only be escaped through detaching from source of the distress.

The key is to remember that despite your circumstances, one always has the fundamental choice to choose how one reacts to those circumstances. Despair and depression are not inevitable. You have the inner power to choose hope over despair, and inner joy over depression.

As the weeks passed, I learned that my old friend was gravely ill and in fact dying.

Too ill to continue running the restaurant, I stopped calling on Joel and weeks later, while servicing another restaurant account, learned that Joel had passed on. Upon hearing this, I decided to visit his wife.

"Catherine, please accept my sincerest condolences for your loss. Joel was a wonderful man and will be dearly missed," I began.

"His passing was so sad and so untimely. He was in the prime of life. I just don't understand why things like this happen," Catherine shared from deep in her heart, after giving me a warm hug.

"There is nothing I can say to console you, however it is a walk we will all take sooner or later," I offered, trying to sensitively validate her grief.

"David, you will never know how much you helped us through this difficult period," Catherine added.

"Well, if that's true, I am grateful for anything I may have done to make Joel's last days more peaceful."

I wasn't sure what she meant at first, because I hadn't seen them for months. After some thought, I realized that perhaps what had helped them was my passing on the concept of *choices*. Again, we never know what gifts we have to offer. Pass them on and good things can happen.

Walking away from that poignant conversation, I began to realize the potency of that important principal of Fundamental Choices in shaping our lives and attitudes. For seven years I continued working, selling wine, learning more about what I had to offer, and shaping my new gifts before facing my next greatest life-changing challenge.

When the inevitable corporate downsizing led to a layoff, I found myself once again struggling to regain my footing. Being suddenly unemployed was nearly as life altering as my stroke.

After recovering enough function to get back to work, the comfort of returning to the daily routine of getting up and heading for the office, earning an income, paying bills, restored that important sense of normalcy despite my physical disability. Now, unemployed for the first time in my life, the impact of being disabled was magnified.

Used to earning an upper five-figure income, my first inclination was to interview for similar positions with other companies. Repeated rejections forced me to consider other options. Could losing my job become another blessing? Experiences like the one I had with Joel made me realize that by simply sharing the insights learned through my stroke, I could make a difference in the lives of others. What could I do professionally to build on the spiritual momentum becoming more and more important in my life?

Could being without a job become an opportunity? If so, where could it lead? Adopting that attitude in a time of adversity can open up a Universe of possibilities. Such life-altering transitions take time. Without a job, I now had the time to contemplate those possibilities. It required a huge leap of Faith to believe that a better Path at this time in my life might not involve the steady employment and high salary I was used to.

6

PHYSICIAN, HEAL THYSELF

As I open this door, may I be open to allowing all possibilities to be brought to me. I ask to be receptive to whatever and whoever comes my way this glorious day.

On this sunny, warm, summer late morning in May, three people walked through my Pop More Corks doors. After some preliminary conversation it became apparent that these were professionals in the health care field. The women were therapists. It didn't take long before one of them noticed I was struggling with my movement and surmised I was dealing with the aftermath of a stroke.

"You seem to be doing quite well. When did you have your stroke?" Denise began.

"Let me think . . . nine years ago," I answered.

"You must be pleased with your progress. Many aren't so fortunate after a stroke," she added.

"I know you're right, and I do try to remember that when things get tough for me from time to time," I agreed.

"So, is this your store?" her friend, Rebekha asked.

"Yes it is," I proudly admitted.

"When did you open the store?" the third woman, Rose, asked.

"About a year ago. Would you be interested in sharing some wine with me today?" I asked.

"Yes, indeed," Rose answered, speaking easily for the group after seeing everyone's eyes light up at my suggestion.

"This Gazela Vinho Verde is from the Vinho Verde region in far northern Portugal, right where it borders with Spain. It can be made out of up to ten different grape varieties, although, this particular one is made from two, Albarino, and Loureiro. Looking at the wine, what color do you see?" I asked.

"Certainly not red," Rose replied.

"A pale lime, if anything," Rebekha added.

"Very good! Verde means 'green' in Portuguese and, indeed, you are seeing a greenish cast as the wine's color. It is a light, crisp style of white wine with some spritzy characteristics. It's not at all a sparkling wine like a Champagne or Cava, but it has some effervescence. Portugal is known for warm summers, and if you visit during a hot spell, you'll see many of the people sitting around in the shade drinking Vinho Verde. And so, this refreshing Gazela Vinho Verde would be an excellent choice on a hot summer day, sitting around the pool or out on the beach to quench your thirst and enhance your appreciation of whatever you're doing.

"Being lower in alcohol, at about nine percent, this wine could be chosen specifically for the fact that it is not as intoxicating as a normal wine. For that reason, it might be preferred to serve at a luncheon or earlier in the day. Even after a couple of glasses, you'll still be able to function and go on with your day. This Gazela Vinho Verde would go well with any light appetizers, like a shrimp cocktail or raw vegetables and dip. On to California for the next wine.

"Lou Preston is a wonderful gentleman who lives in the Dry Creek Valley of Sonoma County in California. I've been associated with him, selling his wines, for over 20 years. His Preston Sauvignon Blanc is made entirely from grapes grown in his 100% certified organic vineyards. I only get about 15 cases of his wine each year and it sells out in a month or so. I would order more if it were possible.

As it is, I get most of his wine that comes into Wisconsin. He only sells to five states.

"Today we're tasting his 2006 Sauvignon Blanc. Each spring the previous year's vintage becomes available. It doesn't see any barrel fermentation or barrel aging, so it's all about the fruit flavors and does display the Dry Creek Valley classic herbal, grassy somewhat medium bodied character along with some melon, citrus, and grapefruit tones. It's a great wine to go with chicken, or fish."

"You mentioned it was organic. Does that affect the wine one way or the other in your opinion?" Denise asked.

"In this case, without a doubt, the organic processing has led to an outstanding wine with excellent character."

"Does that mean there are no sulfites in the wine?" Rebekha wondered.

"It's impossible for a wine not to have sulfites. To make wine, grape juice is fermented. In that process, yeast converts sugar into alcohol, carbon dioxide, and among many other products, sulfites are generated. Being organic, this Dry Creek Valley Sauvignon Blanc does not have any extra added sulfites to extend the shelf life, unlike the policy of many of the larger wineries."

"Does that explain why at times you do and at times you don't see the word 'sulfites' on the label?" Rose questioned.

"Some will say, 'Contains Added Sulfites' and those will be your mass produced corporate wineries. Because they are producing hundreds of thousands of cases, they add sulfites to keep the wine stable over long periods of time. Other labels will say, 'Contains Sulfites' which means that the levels of sulfites have reached the point where by law they have to be listed on the label. When you find a wine where sulfites are not listed anywhere on the label, that simply means that the sulfite level is below that legal standard. Next, let's taste a red wine from Bordeaux, the far southwestern region of France.

"Known for their quality wines, this region along the banks of the Dordogne River in Bordeaux empties into the Gironde estuary leading to the Atlantic Ocean. They can be blended with up to five different grape varieties; Cabernet Sauvignon, Cabernet Franc, Petite Verdot, Malbec, and Merlot. Whereas any of these five can be used, the majority of wines coming from this region are based on either Cabernet Sauvignon or Merlot. The blend is determined by where in Bordeaux the wine is produced.

"On the left side of the Gironde estuary, called the Left Bank of Bordeaux, most of the wines primarily use the Cabernet Sauvignon grape. One of the famous wines from this region is Chateaux Mouton Rothschild, which sells for $200 - $300 a bottle. This next wine comes from the right bank of Bordeaux, an area called Fronsac. This sub district of the right bank produces wines using mainly the Merlot grape variety.

"Although this Chateaux Barrail Chevrol is made primarily of Merlot grapes, it has a surprisingly different flavor profile from, say, a California, Australian, or Washington State Merlot. As is always the case, grapes grown in a specific region of the world will have unique characteristics. In Bordeaux Merlot grapes have an earthy, herbal tone, and come across as being dryer and less fruit forward compared to a California Merlot. I would serve this wine with a hearty beef stew or a tender slice of juicy rare prime rib. It wonderfully represents the style of wine that comes from the right bank of the Bordeaux in Fronsac. For our next selection, we go to Italy.

"In Tuscany, we're going to the most famous region, Chianti Classico, where by law, a wine made from this area must use at least 85% Sangiovese grapes. Traditionally, to call a wine, Chianti Classico, there were also restrictions on the other grapes used. Typically, Caniaolo, Colorino, and even a white grape variety, Trebbino, were allowed in the blend with Sangiovese grapes. Then, 15-20 years ago some blends using Merlot, Syrah, or Cabernet Sauvignon made a softer, less rustic Chianti Classico with a wider appeal. As a result, the law was changed to allow other grape varieties in the Chianti Classico blend.

"Chianti Classico now comes in two broad general styles, the old fashioned, more rustic blend using the traditional grape varieties, and the newer softer more modern blend of Chianti Classico. Wines from the Chianti Classico region have risen in fame and often are more expensive. However, I've found some less expensive wines with a similar style, but which do not originate from this Chianti Classico region.

"The actual wine we're tasting today, a Barco Reale di Carmingano, is from Italy, from Tuscany, but from an area in Tuscany just outside of the Chianti Classico region, in an area called Carmingano. The rules for Carmingano wines are similar to those for Chianti Classico in that 85% of the blend must be Sangiovese, but years ago the wineries began growing Cabernet Sauvignon grapes in their area and blending that variety with the Sangiovese grapes. Because of their location, you can get a wonderful bottle of Chianti Classico style wine for $15.99 as opposed to spending $25 or $30 for an actual Chianti Classico."

"I've been to a few Italian restaurants and was always offered Chianti as a wine to have with dinner. Why is that?" Denise wondered.

"A Chianti goes well with a pasta and red sauce or Tuscan grilled meats, or even a good pizza because it has some acidity along with a dryer, rustic, earthy character that matches up wonderfully with the acidity and sweetness in a good Italian pasta sauce. To finish up today's tasting we're going back to a sweeter white wine, and we're moving on to Germany."

"I'll bet you're going to mention the Rhine River," Rebekha guessed as I poured out the samples.

"You are absolutely correct! There are two main rivers flowing through Germany along which grapes are grown. One grape growing region is the Moselle River Valley while the other is along the Rhine. The wine we're tasting today, a Piesporter Michelsberg Riesling Spatlese, comes from the Moselle River Valley. As with many German wines, this Piesporter Michelsberg Riesling Spatlese is made from the Riesling grape variety. Often, there is so much information given in the name of a wine.

"On the banks of the Moselle River is a town called, Piesport. Outside of that town, there is a vineyard area called, Michelsberg, and in that vineyard area they grow Riesling grapes. The word, Spatlese, refers to the sweetness level of the grapes when they were picked. If you find these words, Kabinett, Spatlese, Auslese, Berenauslese, or Trockenberenauslese, in order, they refer to the sweetness of the wine, with Trockenberenauslese being the sweetest designation. What flavors are coming through as you taste this wine?" I asked the group.

"I get the sweetness, but it's certainly not an overly sweet dessert style wine, just like you said," was Rebekha's comment.

"I'm getting some fruit, but I'm not sure which," Rose added.

"How about some apple flavor?" Denise suggested.

"Absolutely, apple is a distinctly crisp, clean, and consistent fruit flavor of this Piesporter Michelsberg Riesling Spatlese," I shared.

"So, how do the producers control the sweetness level in their wines?" Rose asked.

"During fermentation, the yeast is consuming the sugars in the grape juice. To produce a completely dry wine, the yeast is allowed to use up all the sugar. For sweeter wines, the fermentation process is stopped before that stage is reached," I replied.

"And how would you serve this wine?" Rebekha wondered.

"This wine would be good to serve as a cocktail alone, or as an after dinner sipping wine."

"We're going to buy some wine, but first we want to walk around and see the sights. Would that be all right?" Rose asked.

"I noticed you all rode up on bikes. You're more than welcome to leave them in the courtyard, walk around, and pick them up later," I offered, realizing from the conversation that this was their first time in the quaint resort town of Lake Geneva.

"That would be great," Rebekha answered.

"And, can we leave our backpacks with the bikes?" Denise followed.

"Not a problem. I'll keep an eye on everything while you're gone," I answered.

Having heard some of the details of my difficult path back from a stroke, the looks on the ladies' faces spoke volumes of praise and amazement for such a story.

From seven years back when I returned to the 9-5 rat race, to losing my job, to having a problem finding a new position, to opening up Pop More Corks with all that entails, carrying out all the daily demanding activities with only one functioning arm and leg, comprised a story of recovery the likes of which our three therapists had never seen before.

They suspected there must be a unique factor involved and they wanted to know what it was, but that might have to wait for another day.

So the ladies left and I mulled over some things I was hoping to have a chance to say when they returned.

I spent most of my professional life in the business sector where the overriding goal was simply to generate as much profit as possible. After my stroke, I became familiar with a different type of professional.

Yes, they earned a salary, but their lives were dedicated to the service of others. Such professionals, like the ones who helped me fight back from the effects of my stroke, opened my eyes to a new standard of professionalism. A few hours later, the ladies returned.

"Before you leave, I just had to let you know how much I appreciate the work you do," I began.

"Not that we expect compliments, but they are always appreciated," Rose replied.

"Rehabbing in the hospital, I met quite a few like you three, and they truly made a difference in my life," I added.

"So often, our patients help us as much as we help them," Denise added.

"That is true," Rebekha said.

"Well, ladies, once again, thank you for being who you are," were my parting words as the ladies gathered their things, mounted their bikes, and left Pop More Corks.

*P*arable *R*eflections

As they rode off, I couldn't help but remember my personal rehabilitation struggle. Right after my stroke I was lying flat on my back and couldn't move my arm or leg even a fraction of an inch. Yes, my therapists always predicted a positive outcome during their sessions with me, but there was more than medical science accounting for what was happening and they were the first to admit it.

After my therapy was completed, several confided that though they initially didn't see many signs of hope for a substantial recovery, they could see something extremely substantial in me that they knew would allow me to realize whatever recovery potential was possible. It was a joint effort as is every successful rehabilitation outcome.

Trained professional intervention was critical to my successful rehabilitation, however, doctors are not responsible for the patient's wellness—that is each and every patient's responsibility. The professionals use their tools to light the way, but each patient must walk the path to health and wellness alone.

As the Pop More Corks clock reached 7:00 PM, once again it was time to close and lock the doors. Key in hand, I thought my evening mantra.

As I close this door, I am thankful for all the wonderful people and experiences that have been brought to me this day.

7

EMBRACING CHANGE

After seven years of making a significant contribution to the company's bottom line, despite the physical limitations from my stroke, and not because of these limitations, I found himself, like so many millions of other American workers, caught in the cold, heartless corporate vise of downsizing. When the bean counters get done, it's only about the bottom line and never about the real people and lives that get shredded.

New management determined that my position was one of many no longer considered critical to the continued success of the company. Just laid off, 51 years old, used to a substantial income, divorced, living in what was supposed to be a temporary residence, I was feeling anything but secure about my future. My plan was to find a similar position somewhere within the wine industry.

There were opportunities. In the Chicago area were winery jobs and other distribution companies but, although the interviews seemed to go well, there were few callbacks and no job offers. By law, having a disability can not be a reason to be refused a job, but it became apparent my disability was a factor. The problem was company health insurance.

No personnel director would ever admit this, but health insurance costs being what they are, and knowing they would have to offer me insurance, the cost profile made that prohibitive. In many cases, I was well qualified or even overqualified for positions, and yet not offered the job. Soon, my severance package ran out and I had no money coming in. Facing the prospect of not being able to find a job, I considered trying to qualify for Social Security disability supplemental income.

Initial interviews revealed the critical fact that I had been gainfully employed for seven years despite the disability I now asserted was keeping me from finding work. I was forced to go back to my rehabilitation team and ask to have my current ability to function retested so I could present current data for my Social Security application.

Because of my successful job performance during the past seven years, my rehab team gave me little hope that my disability claim would be processed. Although there is a list of conditions that automatically qualify a person for disability compensation, the professionals handling my application were not about to volunteer that information.

I did my homework and learned that anyone with two limbs functioning below a certain percentage standard automatically qualified for supplemental income. During a subsequent interview, I presented my findings and my claim was accepted. Social Security policy controls costs by not being generous with their compensation assistance. The same can be said for the medical insurance industry which is, unfortunately, a business first and foremost.

A claim denied, boosts the company's bottom line, whether the claim for service is justified or not. It is the responsibility of every claimant to do their homework and not take no for an answer. With some money coming in now, I had a chance to reflect on my situation and begin to conceive of a radical new direction in my professional life.

Although I was a wine expert who had worked for years in the wine distribution industry, although I had called on many wine stores and restaurants, I'd never thought of owning my own business in order to capitalize on my expertise. During an eight month period in which my job prospects declined along with my income, I began to believe that owning and operating my own business might be my best option to resume a fruitful professional life.

8

SPREADING THE GOOD NEWS

As I open this door, may I be open to allowing all possibilities to be brought to me. I ask to be receptive to whatever and whoever comes my way this glorious day.

"David, how about placing an ad in our charity cookbook this year," JoAnn began, the first person through the door on a brand new Monday morning in May.

"Sure, I'll do an ad," I replied, feeling more and more a part of the group of longtime Lake Geneva merchants.

"Wonderful! My friend, Marlene, will be in to talk about the particulars. Welcome aboard and, thanks!" JoAnn responded.

A couple days later, Marlene came in and during a relatively short conversation, without talking about anything to do with God or religion, we worked out the details of the Pop More Corks ad.

Before leaving she turned back to me and said, "I see you're doing the Work of my Father in this place."

"What do you mean?" I asked.

"I'm not a religious person, but you made me feel warm, valued, and cared for. Thank you very much," were Marlene's heartfelt comments.

*P*arable *R*eflections

The core of any faith is to be able to reach out in love to the people around you through opening your heart to the love the Greater Power has to share with all of us.

My daily intention to be of service, to be open, was once again honored. As a blessing, a special soul was sent to share her reaction to my intention. In the Hindu tradition, a guest, someone known, or a stranger, would be treated as a visiting deity, as an expression and extension of the creative power that gifted each of us with life.

During my daily morning intention, I am acutely aware that I am not alone—that with the help of the Greater Power, interactions that serve the greater good can take place in my wine shop. For that to happen, I consciously become open for that power to work through me. When I open that channel, a palpable energy fills the space, sharing a prominent role with my words about wine in creating the potential for a mutually meaningful experience at Pop More Corks.

As the Pop More Corks clock reached 7:00 PM, once again it was time to close and lock the doors. Key in hand, I thought my evening mantra.

As I close this door, I am thankful for all the wonderful people and experiences that have been brought to me this day.

9

POP MORE CORKS, INCORPORATED

Living in Genoa City, I was a regular visitor to the quaint resort town of Lake Geneva, Wisconsin. As most every visitor does, one day in the fall of 2005, I found myself walking by a florist shop located in the northeast end of downtown. A sign in their window indicated they were going out of business. I walked in to find out more. Looking around with both my eyes and my imagination wide open, the idea for Pop More Corks was conceived.

Some galvanized ice buckets were for sale. I saw them holding ice and chilling wine bottles, and purchased them. I also noticed a long stained glass welcome sign featuring grape leaves and thought that I would also need such a sign for my wine store. Being unemployed, money was tight and I had to pass on the sign, but I learned who the landlord was and walked out the door that day thinking I'd just found a great location to open a wine store. Before I could take the next step, a tragic misstep almost ended the dream before it began.

On the way to visit a friend, lifting myself and a couple of heavy bundles up some icy steps, I lost my balance, fell, and fractured my hip. Unable to move, in severe pain, I managed to get out my cell phone and called into the house for help. Some coaxing to get up from well meaning neighbors proved fruitless. Paramedics were called and subsequent X-rays confirmed a broken right hip.

Placed in traction, consultations recommended hip replacement surgery. It was expensive, but I'd kept up my health insurance at a cost of $900 a month. I bore the expense because one has to be on disability for two years before qualifying for Medicare if you're under 65. The surgery went well and I went back to the rehabilitation center to rebuild leg function with my new hip.

Having learned a number of crisis-coping skills during my hospital stays, I slipped right back into the routine and completed my rehabilitation in two weeks. Three more months passed just getting back to normal, with a couple more needed to build up the strength to resume plans to open my wine store.

Finally ready to take the next step, and reasonably good in matters of finance, I began developing an informal business plan involving monthly expenses and projected income. Unable to fund a payroll for employees, I expected to be on my own. Before opening Pop More Corks, a part-time position in sales at a wine store provided some much needed experience.

Ideas for shelving were passed on to a friend who would construct them when the time came to renovate the flower shop space. From my association with the wine store owner, I learned many of the business aspects of running such an operation. Most of all, I realized I could manage the physical requirements of managing a wine shop. During this period, I incorporated Pop More Corks as a wine consulting business.

Pop More Corks, as a retail operation, represented the restoration of my professional dignity, a return to a more normal life of resuming my role as a productive member of the professional community, it involved an area in which I was an expert, and physically it was something I knew he could handle. Having the idea was one thing, making it happen would prove to be a considerable challenge, but once again, the power of Synchronicity began to open doors.

My intention firmly in place, but not at all sure where the money for the store would come from, I found myself visiting my father in Texas, after my mother passed away.

My father was a musician, an accordion player, and often entertained in nursing homes and hospitals accompanied by a violin player, a close and dear friend who came into his life after his wife died. The two were inseparable.

When illness forced his friend to move to Michigan for the support of her family, it didn't take much coaxing for me to encourage my father to sell his condo and relocate, returning to his childhood hometown to be with several other family members including his sister, two brothers, and me, and nearer to his dear friend now living in Michigan. Upon learning of my wish to open Pop More Corks in Lake Geneva, he didn't hesitate to lend his support.

Without being gainfully employed, normal channels for business loans, even ones based on the equity in my home, were not within the realm of possibility. With the financing in place, I was able to begin serious preparations to open Pop More Corks.

The day before the Pop More Corks grand opening, after many hours making final preparations, while turning to lock the front door, noticing my stained glass sign triggered a vivid memory of the day I first walked into the space that would become Pop More Corks.

That sign I couldn't afford to buy for my store, the one I saw the day I walked into the florist shop, is now hanging in the entrance hall, but not because I purchased it. One of the wine salesmen I did business with, a good friend who shared my dream to open a wine concession some day, purchased the sign before Pop More Corks opened and later, seeing the need, offered to let me use the sign indefinitely.

My dream to own and run my own wine store became a reality in August of 2006. The donated stained glass sign was just one of many acts of collective goodwill, kindness, and support from a number of friends and family who believed in my dream.

*P*arable *R*eflections

In a very real sense, I've seen that when we help others, we help ourselves. We are all connected through a Karmic reality that operates to promote generosity, kindness, understanding, and compassion in the daily world we live in.

After one year in operation, the unique wine culture experience to be found at Pop More Corks continues to be enjoyed by more and more loyal customers as they share their experience through word-of-mouth recommendations.

I had been in the business world and in sales long enough to understand the role that relationships play building a client base. I strive to relate to each and every customer who honors me by walking through the Pop More Corks doors in such a way that they will tell someone else something about their experience. If that happens, I have done my job, honoring my calling to serve—not only a good wine, but something more to refresh the soul's palate.

10

THE GIFT OF FAMILY

As I open this door, may I be open to allowing all possibilities to be brought to me. I ask to be receptive to whatever and whoever comes my way this glorious day.

I had seen John before. Several times he'd come into Pop More Corks alone. I'd also noticed John with his daughter, Melanie, and their border collie, Rex, meandering along Lake Geneva's downtown and lakefront sidewalks. They weren't easy to miss or forget. John would typically be pushing a stroller carrying Melanie, who at 21 looked no more than the size of a typical four-year-old child.

Melanie was anything but typical and yet John seemed very much like a typical dad proudly heading up a normal American family.

On this remembered day, John had Melanie and Rex with him as he approached Pop More Cork's front door.

"Come in . . . come in . . . everyone is welcome!" I warmly beckoned, waving the threesome inside to the Pop More Corks foyer.

"Are you sure? My dog can get a bit rambunctious around people," John cautioned.

"He won't be a problem. I've got treats and a bowl of water for him. What's his name, anyway?" I asked while moving toward the bowl I kept under the counter for just such occasions.

"Rex is a good old dog. I've had him for nine years now. He's been a big help with my daughter, Melanie," John added.

The intelligent border collie seemed to know when he was the subject of any conversation and reacted by spinning in several circles, yawning that typical jaw-stretching nervous yawn, before sitting at John's feet. Melanie was another story. She wasn't making a sound, moving much, or reacting to anything being said.

"So, this is your daughter?" I asked.

"Yes, this is my precious Melanie, my youngest. We have two older boys, but they've both left the nest already."

So as not to exclude Melanie, who was actually 21 years old, but severely underdeveloped, deaf and mute because of a childhood illness, John accompanied his words to me with sign language within comfortable sight of his daughter.

"Hello Melanie," I said, speaking in her direction, but not sure how to effectively communicate with her.

"So, what brings you to town today?" I inquired, turning back to John.

"Just need to pick up some white wine for a fish dinner my wife is planning this evening," John replied.

"I just happen to have several excellent white wines open. These four are all made from the same Pinot Grigio grape variety, but because they are grown in different parts of the world, the resulting wines will taste very differently. One of the more popular types of white wines from Italy is made from the Pinot Grigio grape. I've mentioned before that many Old World wines, such as those from France, Spain, and Italy, have names that reflect where it comes from. As is the case with all things involving wine, there are exceptions to every rule. The convention for these white wines is to name the wine after the grape, Pinot Grigio. There is one thing you can be sure of, however. In Europe, if the name of a grape variety is on the label, by law the wine must be made entirely of that type of grape. The requirement varies according to the region; California requires at least 75% of the grape variety listed on the label be used to produce the wine."

"Why is it that sometimes I see Pinot Grigio on a label and at other times I see Pinot Gris?" John asked.

"Again, these wines are made from the same Pinot Grigio/Pinot Gris grape. The name used will be dependent upon the origin of the grapes. In Italy, Argentina, and California you will often see the word Pinot Grigio. Yet in Alsace, France or in Oregon they can be named, Pinot Gris. In both cases, they are wines made from exactly the same grape variety. This first Pinot Grigio is from Italy, from the Veneto, a broad, lush, flat, well watered river valley with rich black loam soil ideal for growing, farming, and harvesting grapes. These agricultural benefits actually present somewhat of a problem for the producers.

"When vines grow full and tall, too much of the plant energy can go into the plant vegetation at the expense of the fruit. When vines are planted in areas where they have some difficulty thriving, the plant's response to being concerned about its survival is to put more energy into the reproductive system, into the grapes. This results in grapes with more intensity on struggling vines. Getting back to this Pinot Grigio from the Veneto, it is a good wine, but not what would be described as complex. The Veneto is a warm region where the grapes tend to ripen fully, producing a broader mouth feel when you taste the wine. For example, this Sartori Pinot Grigio from the Veneto is simple, soft, round, and easy drinking, a nice everyday style of white wine from northern Italy," I explained as I poured a sample into John's glass.

"I like this. I suppose I could say it tastes simple, but it is good. What's next?" John asked while continuing to swirl the Sartori and sniff the aromas wafting up from his glass.

"This next wine is also a Pinot Grigio, but originates from the Trentino, an even more northern region and much more hilly, bordering on mountainous. The grapes can be grown on the valley floor, known as Trentino Val d'Adige, leading to the Alps, or up the hillsides, in a region named Trentino Alto Adige. This Gaierhof Pinot Grigio comes from the Trentino Alto Adige region. What you'll notice immediately is the wine's crispness. The climate is cooler, keeping the grapes from getting overly ripe. They present a clean, refreshing acidity and mineral character resulting from a cooler climate and thinner soil. Because of the growing environment, it is a more complex style of wine with layered flavors," I shared, as John sampled the wine.

"I do like this one better," John said.

"For this next wine we will be crossing the Atlantic on our way to the United States and to Oregon to taste a Pinot Gris from the Willamette Valley produced by the Ponzi Vineyards. For well over 25 years they've led the way in managing their hillside vineyards in a sustainable manner. As good stewards of the land, they use little or no pesticides or herbicides. They were one of the first wineries to produce a quality Pinot Gris in Oregon. Although the Willamette Valley is certainly cooler than any climate in California, conditions tend to be warmer than the Trentino in Italy. This New World wine from a warmer climate will fill your mouth with broader, fruit-forward flavors. All four of the wines we're tasting today were fermented in stainless steel containers and so the pure Pinot Grigio/Pinot Gris grape flavors are uncomplicated with oak barrel aging. Tasting these wines side by side, I hope you can see how different they are despite all being fermented from the same Pinot Grigio/Pinot Gris grape variety, and all because of the characteristics of the land where the grapes were grown," ended my remarks about the first four wines.

"You made your case well and the samples confirmed everything you said," John agreed while picking up the rich, broad, mouth-filling, fruit flavors that came across as sweeter even without any more residual sugars.

"The last wine, a Monte Volpe Pinot Grigio is from Mendocino County in California. Mendocino County is north of Napa Valley and that's good because Pinot Grigio grapes don't like a climate that is too warm. Although these hillside vineyards are cooler than those in Napa Valley or Sonoma County, they are certainly warmer than those in the Willamette Valley in Oregon. So, because of the warmer climate, this Monte Volpe Pinot Grigio will present with even more rich fruit, more body, and more weight than the Pinot Gris from Oregon. The Monte Volpe winery specializes in Italian varieties of wines produced from grapes grown in the Mendocino area of California.

"All the wines we've tasted would serve well as cocktail wines, enjoyed and appreciated by themselves, but certainly, for example, the Trentino Pinot Grigio with its mineral base, would go well with a cream sauce pasta dish where its crispness could cut through the weight of the sauce of a Fettuccini Alfredo. The Ponzi Pinot Gris would complement a lighter fish dinner as in, perhaps, a sautéed walleyed pike or maybe a grilled trout."

"Would this evaluation strategy of tasting wines made from the same grape apply to other grape varieties?" John wondered.

"Certainly, in fact, tasting several wines made from the same grape variety, but grown in different parts of the world is an excellent way to determine, first of all, what type of grape you prefer, and secondly, what region in the world you prefer the grapes in your wine to come from," I suggested.

"John, you've been in a few times before, but I don't think I know what you do for a living," I inquired, as John sipped the final Monte Volpe Pinot Grigio and smiled with approval.

"I keep track of all the things our government buys to supply our troops. Database management, I guess is what you'd call it," John replied.

"Sounds like a major responsibility."

"I suppose it is, but to me it's just a file on a computer screen and that's what I've been trained to understand and work with," John humbly added.

"I didn't think there were any big government warehouses in this area," I added.

"That's perceptive of you. No, there aren't. The facility I manage is in Nevada. My schedule varies, but typically I'm there a week on, then a week off, or if there's more to do, two weeks on and two weeks off."

"How does that work for you?" I empathetically asked.

"It's not bad. Anyway, I've gotten used to it, but I don't like being away from the family for that long," John admitted while petting Rex who had snuggled up to his left leg, and stroking Melanie's hair with his other hand.

"I'm calling up images from the end of, *Citizen Kane*, the Orson Wells film about William Randolph Hearst the newspaper magnate. At the end of his life, all of his belongings were burning in a huge storage facility along with an American Flyer sled with the name, Rosebud, painted on it," I shared.

"I've seen that film, too, and that space won't quite do. Think instead of the final scene from *Raiders of the Lost Ark* where the Ark of the Covenant was nailed into a common wooden crate and buried deep inside a gigantic government building," John suggested.

Melanie wasn't really following the conversation, yet she was capable of doing so and given her malady she was rather high functioning with her mental and emotional level at that of a 3rd or 4th grader. John noticed Melanie daydreaming. We soon got back to our conversation about just the right white wine for family fish dinner when John noticed again that his daughter was fidgeting.

"Well, David, I hate to cut this short, but I can see that Melanie has had enough and wants to get going."

"Not a problem. As always, thanks for coming, and in the future please don't hesitate to bring Melanie and Rex with you!" were my parting words as I took the twenty dollar bill and passed John a special bottle of Monchoff Riesling to take home.

John gathered his daughter and faithful dog and left for another extended leisurely walk along the calming Lake Geneva shoreline. It was apparent to me that John's dreams are fulfilled through his committed love for his family. It was also apparent that Melanie's medical or developmental issues had no bearing on his dedication or feelings of deep inner joy generated by his role as provider and protector of his family.

*P*arable *R*eflections

All life is a Gift. All human life is precious. Our capacity to love has no bounds and can defy explanation. The term "disability" is merely a crude reference to the fact that someone is experiencing limitations. What the term does not explain is the fact that a disability need not diminish the fundamental value of the person who continues to honor the Gift of life by not giving up on life as a result of their struggle.

We all carry some burden, at times obvious, often hidden, and despite that burden, we can and must carry on and continue to work out the great search for Truth that takes place each and every day we are blessed to breathe on this Earth.

Although, to some, Melanie might be considered a burden, John and his wife are delighted for the special gift of having her in their lives and will lovingly care for Melanie as long as they are able.

As the Pop More Corks clock reached 7:00 PM, once again it was time to close and lock the doors. Key in hand, I thought my evening mantra.

As I close this door, I am thankful for all the wonderful people and experiences that have been brought to me this day.

11

METAPHYSICIAN, HEAL THYSELF

Following my stroke, I was thoroughly informed about the medical, physical, and rational aspects of my condition. The plan for my rehabilitation was laid out and I dove in 100% committed to the process. My days were heavily structured leaving me little free time to contemplate the emotional wounds I'd suffered along with the stroke.

In the painful quiet of my room at night, I began to confront the metaphysical complications of my stroke. A sick soul will not allow a sick body to heal. I understood the potential dangers of allowing feelings of deep regret, bitterness, or anger to fester for any length of time.

My team of doctors and therapists were providing the medical resources needed to heal my body. It soon became apparent that it wasn't going to be enough to invest my efforts only in the prescribed rehabilitation activities. Wanting to bring whatever Greater Powers there were to bear on a holistic healing effort, I began searching through my considerable collection of spiritually centered materials.

Over the years, I'd acquired a number of resources centering around spirituality. Using them, I began a study designed to help heal my soul of the emotional trauma caused by the stroke. The first resource I tapped into was a book of spiritual concepts, reviewed and explained in sacred texts from all the world's great religions. I needed to make sense of what happened and draw on unifying sources of spiritual strength during the process of recovery.

Hoping to harness the energies that fuel the soul and apply them to my rehabilitation, I turned to a variety of sources for information and inspiration. Having been grounded in the Episcopalian tradition, I understood the basics of Christian teachings. I was familiar with the potential role of suffering as a key to unlock certain kinds of wisdom. I was taught about the possibility of being reborn into a new life of spiritual awareness.

I realized my condition was serious and that recovery would require only the most serious commitment of all available resources. Despite what appeared to be a terrible personal tragedy, almost immediately there were hints that something was there—something I was going to be able to tap into—sources of spiritual energy I possibly was aware of earlier, but not forced to recognize and make use of until the stroke hit.

Before the stroke, I'd been drawn to material about Buddhism, had done some meditating, and had already accepted the reality of a Higher Power. Having the belief was one thing, now I had to act on those beliefs and have faith that summoning healing energies from spiritual sources would indeed make a difference.

Shakti Gawain produced a series of tapes explaining the power of meditation to create one's own future realities. Such creative visualization strategies were known to be potent sources of healing. I wasted no time in putting meditative imaging to work remolding my condition. I focused on the key elements, imagining my arm and leg moving again, and my brain's blood vessels performing their functions without bleeds. Combined with everything else I was doing, the results were real and significant.

I wasn't about to stop any one of the therapies and healing strategies I'd committed to. Over time, and with patience, belief, and faith, I began to get better. During daily meditations, I began to understand that the place I'd come to spiritually was a direct result of having had a stroke. I soon began to regard the stroke as a Blessing rather than a personal tragedy.

Besides the creative visualization materials, I was also reading Joseph Campbell's, *The Power of Myth*. That book helped me distill the core spiritual truths and principles from the world's great religions. Proceeding day by day through therapy, finally I was released from the resident rehabilitation program. Before leaving, I arranged to share a meal with everyone on staff who had been instrumental in my recovery. I was so moved by their dedication and contributions I felt the need to offer a perspective on my experience.

"Each and every one of you is incredible. Before coming to this facility, I wasn't aware that there existed so many people from so many different disciplines whose professional lives were so completely dedicated to the service of others. It became obvious to me that your whole reason for being was to help people heal. I came from a world where I was focused only on selling more and more cases of wine, and opening more and more accounts for my company.

"Besides recovering to the point where I could step out into the world again, I've learned some important lessons about how to live in that world. Please don't take this the wrong way, but as important as every physical therapy activity you led me through was, I've never worked harder, or invested more to achieve any goal before in my life.

"I'm only saying this so that you might pass on just how critical it is for the patient to take responsibility for and be completely committed to the whole process of recovery. Much of what I was able to do for myself was a result of reading certain books, and I want you all to have copies" were my closing comments as I passed out the volumes to the appreciation of the assembled group.

*P*arable *R*eflections

There often seems to be a mystical process involved in leading us to the people and information we need at important times in our lives. In my case, it was as if the Universe was aware of where I was headed and began preparing me by bringing books, CD's, and tapes into my life before the stroke. During the recovery process, I would often forgo sleep in order to read and work with the metaphysical resources that were brought to me. Among the most visually colorful, was the Pink Bubble technique.

During the process of creative visualization, one imagines something you want to happen in your future, such as getting out of a wheelchair, and surround the image with a large glossy pink soap bubble. Once securely in the bubble, you send it off into the Universe of possibilities while detaching from the outcome. In his book Joseph Campbell spoke of the spiritual wisdom that has been made available during each age.

Going back through the millennia, avatars have been provided to pass on the spiritual insight that mankind was ready to accept and process. Progressing through the generations, we've come to another great time of transition ushering in a new age. It's time for the entrenched traditions to step aside and make room for new ideas that will bring people together through sharing resources, and live in such a way as to protect the Earth's resources and delicate balance. Among the avatars leading us forward is George Lucas.

His Star Wars Trilogy was a wonderful new myth surrounding an ancient dramatic storyline—a hero must go off and fight the dragon—for it is in the struggle that our souls are refined and tempered in the fires of experience and though the choices that test our values, beliefs, and standards. The surroundings of the journey leading us to confrontations between Good and Evil have certainly changed, but the essence of the struggle remains the same.

Modern new myths, inspired from *Star Wars* and others, such as the *Lord of the Rings* and *Harry Potter*, continue to challenge us to sort out the nature of Good and Evil and find our place in that great fundamental spiritual struggle. Being open to the possibility of being inspired and instructed by many different authors, I kept searching and applying the ideas I was led to.

The ultimate expression of the power of creative visualization was realized when despite all the apparent obstacles, Pop More Corks opened its doors in the fall of 2006. There are great healing and organizing Energies available for our benefit. When we call upon them, drawing them to the service of our needs, it is much more of a channeling process rather than one of gathering or hoarding.

Through meditation and other techniques, one allows the Healing Energy to pass through on its way to helping others.

12

WE ARE NOT IN CONTROL

As I open this door, may I be open to allowing all possibilities to be brought to me. I ask to be receptive to whatever and whoever comes my way this glorious day.

Walking through the Pop More Corks doors, three were browsing the bottles on the shelves before approaching the wine tasting counter. Nothing unusual so far except that collectively they were emotionally spent and seemed to have gone through some ordeal together.

"What brings you to the store today?" I began in typical fashion, while pouring a Spanish cava into their tasting glasses.

"We're visiting family," Sarah answered.

"We're from Burlington," Chandler added.

"Unfortunately, our father is not well and we've all come home to be with him, hoping and praying for the best, but not really expecting any miracles," Carolyn volunteered.

"I'm sorry to hear that," I responded before beginning to share information about the cava they were about to sample.

"We're here to get some wine, go back home, and drown our sorrows . . . how pathetic is that," Sarah admitted, realizing that the relief from their collective grief and sense of impending loss would only be temporary.

"Oh, believe me, I understand. I went through that when my mother passed. It's never easy, but try to give some thought to the good that's coming from the situation," I offered supportively.

"I'm not sure I understand," Carolyn replied.

"Well, first of all, your father's illness brought your family together again. You can make it a precious time to relive the good memories of growing up—of your father raising you," I suggested.

"That's so true. We've already shared a session paging through the family photo album," Chandler added.

"There you go . . . and I'll bet there were even a few smiles to be seen despite what you're going though," I said.

"Yes there were . . . and when we closed the album, it was hard not to feel guilty about having laughed so hard at how we looked and some of the things we'd gotten into during our childhood," Sarah added.

"No need to feel guilty. We'll all walk that lonely road some day. We can't control when or why that will happen to ourselves or to someone we love, but we can control how we react when that time comes," I offered, while pouring a taste of the second wine to be sampled.

"We're at the point where he may not have much time left. We know he'll be gone soon and it's just so hard to accept," Carolyn shared, fighting to hold back the tears that wanted to break through her defenses and express the grief she was feeling

"Of course, you're here primarily to be with your dad, but you're also here for your mom at a time when she needs to have her family around her," I added.

"She hasn't given up hope that dad might recover, and so she hasn't wanted to talk about the changes coming, but we hear you and we're all waiting for the right time to bring up the subject of what options we can offer her if and when she has to go on without him," were Sarah's wise words, speaking for her sisters.

There were signs of the ordeal they were going through. The sisters came into the store without makeup and wearing clothes that looked as if they had been slept in. Their eyes were swollen and bloodshot from crying. The all-night vigils were taking their toll. The wine would hopefully help them temper their grief and linger in a peaceful place for a while before resuming watch at their father's hospice bedside.

The deathwatch had been going on for days, but recent changes in vital signs caused the hospice nurse to pass on that their father would probably be gone by the end of the month. The sisters were feeling uneasy about leaving his bedside, but they all realized they needed some time away to recover from what they'd been through already and gain some strength to be vigilant to the end.

Unable to justify staying away longer, the three sisters left after about an hour. They expected to leave with several bottles of wine. They did not expect to leave having their heavy hearts lightened with the refreshing thought of how it is possible to find good and positive expressions from almost any human experience.

*P*arable *R*eflections

Indeed, the secret to surviving life's hills and valleys, life's triumphs and tragedies—is understanding that we are not in control of much of what happens during our lives, but we are always in control of how we react to what happens.

Our society, our culture, our American values, our institutions lead us to believe that we do or should have control over how our lives unfold. When things happen that are clearly out of our control, the usual emotional response is distress and despair. When our choices, our options are taken away, that's when we can feel life is no longer worth living.

When you're feeling that way, it is always still possible to find Balance. First, recognize that in fact few things in our lives are truly controllable. Next, be willing to give up that control to the Higher Power ultimately responsible for all that happens in our lives and in our world. No matter what happens, gain strength by knowing you are always in control of how you respond—choosing to move forward in hope and gratitude for the possibilities presented by each day of life.

Personal tragedy is different for different people. When people find out some of the details of what I've been through, they often express a feeling that they would never have survived such a personal disaster. Unable to cope in an enlightened way, many mask disaster with some addictive substance or behavior only making matters worse.

I continued to see the three sisters over the next few weeks as their father slowly slipped away. During one visit to Pop More Corks, they brought in their mother. Yes, wine was tasted and talked about, but it became apparent to all that the real reason for their visits was the comfort they left with knowing that even in the midst of a desperately uncontrollable situation, they can always choose hope over despair, joy over sorrow.

I didn't avoid bringing up the difficult subjects or asking the hard questions—one soul who had been there, empathetic to several who were treading that dreaded path of personal loss.

As the Pop More Corks clock reached 7:00 PM, once again it was time to close and lock the doors. Key in hand, I thought my evening mantra.

As I close this door, I am thankful for all the wonderful people and experiences that have been brought to me this day.

13

THE BUSINESS OF BUSINESS

When the Pop More Corks doors close at the end of the day, I reflect not so much on the cash register receipts, but more on the quality of my interactions with customers. There are many places where people can go to purchase a bottle of wine. The key to running a successful business seems to be word-of-mouth referrals and repeat customers.

Business plans for any new company generally do not project a fiscal year-end profit until after the third year of operations. Hopefully during that period, proprietors are building up a client base of loyal customers. A business owner holds on to customers with value and customer service.

It doesn't take much for me to find an excuse to give a customer a discount on their purchase. That means you might be the beneficiary of a returning-customer discount, or a, oh-it's-your-birthday discount, or if you come in on a Tuesday you might get a Tuesday discount—any excuse to make the customer feel they're getting value so they leave feeling valued.

I strive to expose my customers to unique new wines, and work to build up quality, lesser known brands so that my customers can count on a cutting-edge wine tasting experience at Pop More Corks. Moving from wholesale to retail, I understand more than most how pricing and availability affect overall sales.

If you walk into Pop More Corks and browse the shelves you sometimes won't see prices marked on the bottles. By design, I don't want anyone to buy a bottle of wine based solely on price without having an exchange of thoughts and ideas about the wine's best uses, history, and something about the producer.

It's also important that no matter the price, the customer should enjoy the wine when they open it up at home. Wine tasting plays an important role in achieving that goal. When a customer brings a bottle of wine to the counter, it triggers a conversation that thoroughly explores the wine and its intended use.

Through a process like this, any merchant can establish more meaningful relationships with customers and by doing so cultivate a grove of loyal repeat customers.

*P*_{arable} *R*_{eflections}

If one strives not to make money the measure of success, you will nurture a business environment where goodwill leads naturally over time to good profits. Running a successful business does not come without being willing to pay a high personal price. The required investment in time and energy can push a person to the limits of one's ability to function. Profit, of course, is a reality that no thriving business can do without.

In my case, I am more interested in the kind of "prophet" involved in realizing my dream for Pop More Corks—to become a wine store designed to both surprise the palate and refresh the spirits of everyone who walks in.

14

THEY ALL LOVED THE CHINON

As I open this door, may I be open to allowing all possibilities to be brought to me. I ask to be receptive to whatever and whoever comes my way this glorious day.

"My wife is arranging a reception for the French ambassador in Milwaukee at the University Club this weekend. I'm responsible for selecting just the right French red wine for the occasion. Can you help me?" the stressed man inquired with a touch of desperation in his tone as he approached the Pop More Cork's counter.

"Yes I can, and I might add you've come to the right wine shop," I answered with confidence honed from 30 years in the business, but more because this was just the kind of situation where my perspective on wine origins and cultivating the character of unique wines could be appreciated.

"I am so relieved to hear that. I may have been to France, but I am not well versed enough in wines to pick one out for this grand occasion," the man honestly added.

"Well, that's my job, so just help me get started by giving me a few more details," I suggested.

"I'm on a budget, and I can only spend around $35 a bottle, so let's start there."

After discussing a number of possible French wines, I got to thinking about a unique area in France, the Loire Valley, and a red wine named, Charles Jouguet Chinon Cuvee la Terre. The wine was just under $20 a bottle.

"Are you sure this is going to be good enough for such a distinguished gathering," Jack asked, seriously concerned about not disappointing his French wife or any of the dignitaries that would be attending the festivities.

"Trust me, your guests will be pleased with this choice and no one need know how much the wine cost," I said trying to reassure Jack that all would go well at the dinner.

He left with a case of the Chinon without even tasting a sample, based on my recommendation. Three days later, Jack was back.

"I need more Chinon. The size of the party has gone up. I'm upset because I was hoping to have some left over to take home, but it doesn't look like that's going to happen," he added.

I happily supplied Jack with the extra bottles of Chinon. The next day the phone rang.

"David, thank you so much for your recommendation! Everyone loved the Chinon and, of course they all wanted to give me the credit, but as we know, you took the risk and you were so right. There were several wine experts attending, and a number of guests from France, and they were all very impressed with the wine, especially since some mentioned that wines from that region can be uncomplicated and uninteresting. So, thank you, and I'm sure I'll be seeing you again soon," were Jack's complimentary words ending his call.

I was pleased with the kind words, but I understood why the wine was so well received—IT HAD CHARACTER!

The wines at Pop More Corks are chosen because each has a story. Each expresses something of what they're made of, how they're made, who made them, and where they come from. On the other end of the wine

character spectrum, there are wines produced for the mass consumption market, like Kendall-Jackson Chardonnay.

It is a very well made California appellation wine, meaning the winery can use grapes from anywhere in the state of California. The makers can not restrict the brand to a region because of the sophisticated marketing steps used in creating the blend. Surveys begin the process by asking how the consumer wants their chardonnay to taste. From that data a flavor profile will be engineered into the next round of production. The wineries can execute the profile by selecting grapes from throughout California that will result in the blended flavor requested.

This kind of wine exists primarily to make money for the producer. Kendall-Jackson Chardonnay is a good wine. It's just that it has been created to please a broad cross section of the wine-consuming public. The wines selected for the shelves of Pop More Corks have much more unique flavor profiles.

The Chardonnay wines chosen for the inventory represent how a Chardonnay should taste if it comes from a particular region. Chardonnay grapes can be grown in a hundred different places around the world. Chardonnay grapes grown in Santa Barbara county California will taste much different from those grown in the Maconnais in Burgundy in France.

Because the wines speak to not only their type, but where they come from, they have character. Through the experience of a wine tasting, the customer has the opportunity to distinguish these differences. For example, a Chardonnay from the Maconnais in Burgundy in France will taste crisp and clean and very refreshing with no oak to it at all as compared with a big, oaky, buttery Chardonnay from California.

The Chinon I recommended for the French ambassador's event was a red wine from the Chinon district in France produced by Charles Jouguet in the Loire River Valley which runs west of Paris out to the Atlantic Ocean. One of the regions along the river is Chinon. In this area, red wines are made from Cabernet Franc grapes. A Cabernet Franc from this area of France presents a unique flavor profile not found anywhere else in the world.

At any one time there are 400 distinct wines with this quality of character to choose from on the Pop More Corks shelves. They got there through a unique selection process. Having worked in restaurants before my wine wholesaling days, I was familiar with the many different kinds of grapes and where they were grown. I gave a list to my suppliers and asked them to recommend the best representatives of each kind of wine on the list.

Besides promoting the value of character in my wines, by extension, I am celebrating diversity, differences. Every wine from every part of the world has something to offer—something to contribute. Again, by extension, each human being is unique and has something important to add to the tapestry of human experience.

During my young years as a student, I was captivated with geography and thrived on studying about all the remarkably different places and peoples in the world. My passionate interest in wine stemmed from a particular wine's intimate connection to the soil, community, culture, food, people, and climate where the grapes are grown. When a wine tasting dialog begins at Pop More Corks, I use the conversation to travel the globe indulging my delight at the diversity in our world.

*P*arable *R*eflections

There are forces at work trying to homogenize the world for the sake of economy and efficiency. The tendency is for groups to form based on some common set of beliefs. Soon those rigid beliefs build walls keeping others out. Our institutions need to be redesigned to be more inclusive if our world is to have any hope of solving the great global problems we face.

At Pop More Corks, a world of wines rich with diversity and character are valued most. And for the people tasting these celebrated wines, revel in the fact that you are unique in all the world. No matter your profile of personal characteristics, our world would be diminished were you no longer with us.

As the Pop More Corks clock reached 7:00 PM, once again it was time to close and lock the doors. Key in hand, I thought my evening mantra.

As I close this door, I am thankful for all the wonderful people and experiences that have been brought to me this day.

15

WILD FIRES IN WINE COUNTRY

As I open this door, may I be open to allowing all possibilities to be brought to me. I ask to be receptive to whatever and whoever comes my way this glorious day.

During another devastating wave of wildfires in California, three heavy hearted souls walked through the Pop More Corks doors—Hillary was wearing a white knit parka, Janice had on a stylish red hat, and Heidi was sporting a navy blue Nike workout suit. They were from San Diego.

"Can I help you?" I asked.

"Oh, we're just browsing," Janice answered.

From experience, I understood that perhaps they came in because of my sign out front advertising wine tasting and were just a little shy, or they were browsing and looking over the prices on the bottles.

"Do you live in the area?" I followed.

"No, we're from California," came a reply from Heidi who was looking through some of the white wines.

"Well, let me tell you a little bit about the store. Currently I have over 400 wines available and of that number there are about 150 priced under $20. As you browse the shelves you may notice that unless you're really into wines, you're probably not going to recognize many of the labels. Most of what I have you will not see in a grocery store or even in a large liquor store. My wines are all from small producers making only a few thousand cases of individual wines a year.

"The way a wine gets onto my shelves, first of all I have to taste it, secondly I've established a longstanding relationship with the winemakers, the owners, and the producers. I enjoy selling wines where I know those who are actually responsible for production. You can pick any bottle off the shelf and each one has a story, many times it will be a personal story about the individual who made the wine.

"Beyond that, if I can find wines that are organic or biodynamic, that's also important to me because the producers are taking care of their land and taking care of the earth. And, by the way, I do a lot of tasting here. I have several wines open right now and if you would like to share some samples with me, I'd be more than happy to serve them to you," I suggested, having purposely taken the time to ground them in the basic concept that establishes the value of my wine selection.

"We'd love to," was Heidi's reply.

"So, tell me more about California?" I asked while pouring a sample of a Santa Barbara Chardonnay into their glasses.

"I'm afraid where we live, many people have lost their homes to the wildfires raging right now," Janice added.

"I've been following the reports in the news. Have the fires affected you personally?" I inquired.

"We were fortunate. The flames didn't reach our neighborhood," Hillary shared, shaking her head in the sobering realization that it could have been her home that perished in the flames.

"I can only imagine how you felt knowing there wasn't anything you could do to prevent such a personal disaster," I added.

"We were in a mandatory evacuation zone. I remember in the shelter when it hit me that I had absolutely no control over what was going to happen," she went on.

"There is much we can all learn from feelings of helplessness like that. Personal disaster can take many forms and there is no way to completely control our lives so as to remove the risk of such tragedies. Somehow we all must find the strength to go forward afterwards," I suggested, without going into the personal experience of surviving a severe stroke which taught me that important spiritual lesson.

My eyes, now welling up with the uncontrollable tears of deeply felt emotion, met hers and we both understood the depth of the other's experiences although few words were exchanged.

*P*arable *R*eflections

Feelings of being in control about anything, at any time, are an illusion. In fact, when people believe they are in complete control that is often just the time when they will lose something very precious to them. I lived most of my life completely unaware of the arteriole vascular malformation, the AVM, the ticking medical time bomb that was to deliver a personal tragedy into my well ordered life, seemingly under my control.

To varying degrees, every life is visited with similar unexpected setbacks of one sort or another. In the Christian perspective, everyone has a cross to bear. The remarkable paradox is that much good can come from even the worst disaster. Certain kinds of growth it seems can only rise from the ashes of a refining fire. The important point we need to accept is that things will happen beyond our control. After embracing that Truth, what we can and must control is our response to what happens.

In the case of the California wildfires, rising from the ashes of tragedy were many stories of compassion and sharing as those who were able, assisted those who were suffering. And when everyone's immediate needs were taken care of, whole communities accepted the responsibility of the goal of helping to eventually rebuild all the affected homes, often taking great pride when the last home destroyed was finally rebuilt.

Such accomplishments require holding on to hope in the face of tragedy. Having faith that conditions will improve helps a person move past the immediate helpless feelings that follow right after a disaster strikes. Believing the bad that has surfaced can be buried again and covered with better days, tragedy can become a wonderful opportunity to take a fresh look at your life and start anew, helping to define who you are and what you are capable of accomplishing.

The ladies didn't stay long, but when they left, all understood that important ideas and concepts were placed on the wine-tasting table for consideration along with the Santa Barbara Chardonnay.

As the Pop More Corks clock reached 7:00 PM, once again it was time to close and lock the doors. Key in hand, I thought my evening mantra.

As I close this door, I am thankful for all the wonderful people and experiences that have been brought to me this day.

16

GROWING UP EPISCOPALIAN

Growing up Episcopalian didn't provide a meaningful personal spiritual foundation, despite the fact that I was an altar boy. Because of conflicts with clergy, there were often extended periods when my family avoided regular church attendance. The fundamental knowledge and ideas of the Christian faith were, however, firmly implanted. Spirituality had not yet become an integrated part of who I was. What did become integrated was a passion for natural history and geography.

All through childhood, my family traveled, eventually visiting nearly all the states during long road trips. There was a vast diverse natural world beyond the city boundaries of Mundelein, Illinois. I'd seen many depressed areas in the South, driven through Appalachia, the Southwest, seen great rivers, deserts, forests, and the Rocky Mountains. Returning from a trip, I often felt the privilege of my middle class life. For me, studies in school were another way to travel.

I enjoyed geography, social studies, and history the most. Open a geography book and you could virtually visit any country on earth, a social studies book and vicariously experience all the cultures around the world. Just out of college, I began working in a restaurant which is where I met my wife. During a formal date, a bottle of wine was chosen to complement the dinner being served.

It was a Deloach Chardonnay from Sonoma County California. That special wine seemed to christen our relationship. A year later we were married and during a honeymoon excursion we found ourselves in California wine country where that bottle of Deloach Chardonnay came from. Restaurant work proved to be an internship to learn about wine.

Growing more and more curious and interested in wine, in the early 1980's I was given the responsibility of developing a wine list for a restaurant. At that point I dove into the subject with a passion that had been growing steadily. I came up with a list of 150 wines, all from California. This was a unique idea as California wines were struggling to be appreciated along side European wines.

Through purchasing wines for restaurants, and dealing with wine salesmen, I had personal experience with each recommended wine on the list. Following my "bliss" as suggested in, *The Power of Myth*, I next had an opportunity to develop and open a small retail wine store affiliated with the restaurant where I was employed. When the restaurant was sold, I moved the wine store to a new location and took over its ownership and operation.

At that point, my work experience was varied and yet it was clear one of my passionate interests involved wine. The store eventually closed, but led to first a part-time position selling wine, then to my full-time job with Judge & Dolph Ltd.

When a wine became interesting to me, it was often because of how the wine was tied to the grapes grown in a particular region of a country and fermented to complement the food of the culture and people living in that region.

Studying the wines selected for the Pop More Corks inventory is a way for me to continue exploring the people, places, cultures, and food around the world. The more unique the wine, the more interesting were the stories behind the vines, producers, and communities that created the wine.

Growing up Episcopal was just the beginning of a lifelong search for spiritual Truth. My in-depth study of wines eventually led to a study of world cultures, and by extension world religions, which provided the ecumenical foundation for a new passion in my life.

17

"I LEARNED A LOT TODAY"

As I open this door, may I be open to allowing all possibilities to be brought to me. I ask to be receptive to whatever and whoever comes my way this glorious day.

Ralph lived for several years in the heart of French wine country during his adventurous college years. Returning to the States, he brought his love for wine and an appreciation for the best that our wine culture has to offer with him. Settling in the Chicago area, Ralph often had difficulty finding certain wines fondly recalled from his time in France. That problem ended when he walked through the Pop More Corks doors.

"What brings you to Lake Geneva this fine day?" I opened.

"My wife and I have a condo here, so no special reason, to answer your question, but of course, we just love this area and come here whenever we can get away," Ralph answered.

"I must admit, I opened my store here for the same reason."

"I heard the buzz from friends about the new wine shop in town, and had to stop in to check things out for myself. How long has the store been open?" Ralph asked.

"About six months, now. So far so good," I answered.

"Well, I hope I'm not going to prove to be a difficult customer, but I'm having trouble finding a particular French wine. The dealers I've checked with in Chicago haven't been able to help me."

"By all means, do give me a chance! Tell me more about this mysterious wine?"

"I spent a year abroad studying. I was living in France during that period and came to love the wines that were produced in that region. The problem I'm having is finding good representatives of those wines from that period in my life," Ralph shared, hoping this time to be able to "taste" that period in his life without having to fly back to France.

"I have some French wines open. Let's start with these and you can tell me if they measure up to what you remember," I suggested with some confidence realizing they were from a region near the one he was talking about.

From the expression on Ralph's face, I could tell the wines were making the hoped for impression.

"They have an earthy character, but I thought you might like that. You know, try this Samour-Champingy," I added while pouring a sample into Ralph's tasting glass.

Ralph swirled the crimson liquid, examining the depth of color, sniffed the fragrance lofting up, let the wine linger on his palate for a while, then smiled.

"David, that's exactly the quality and type of wine I've been looking for!"

"I'm please you like it and you should, given what I've heard so far. This Samour-Champingy is made from Cabernet-Franc grapes grown in the Loire Valley of France," I added.

From that day on, Ralph was confident in trying the selections I suggested. One day he asked about a particular wine.

"Have you heard of a Domaine Tempier Bandol made from Mouverede grapes?" Ralph asked.

"Yes, I have."

"Can you find it for me?"

"Sure, no problem."

"I hope you can. No one in Chicago has been able to. When I was studying in France I stayed at the Domaine Tempier Winery and, of course, enjoyed many of their fine wines, but their Bandol made a lasting impression. I'm looking forward to tasting it again," Ralph shared.

"Well, I'm sure we can make that happen."

During the next few months, I was able to find a variety of wines from that producer and apparently, from Ralph's reaction, the quality of their wines was still memorable. Over time we explored other unique vintages.

Professionally, Ralph came from the rigorous world of scientific research. A chemist, having written many papers and published articles documenting his projects over the years, he was planning to develop his most promising idea into a book when the call came to take over the University where he already was chair of the research department at the University of Illinois – Chicago, a preeminent research institution.

As chancellor of the university, he was looking forward to a few good years during which he would continue to lead the entire college community toward educational excellence before moving on to the next phase of his life. This was a man who has lived the role of expert and teacher throughout his distinguished career.

Before leaving the store, Ralph passed on a heartfelt, "Thank you so much, I've learned a lot from you."

*P*arable *R*eflections

There is always something we can learn from the people around us. In the broadest spiritual sense, we are not always aware of the experiences and knowledge we need, but walking your Path you'll encounter many different kinds of people at every turn. Be open and share in both directions when the opportunity presents itself. We all have to be willing to take on the roles of both teacher and student.

We all need each other.

We all have something to offer.

When the student is ready, the teacher will appear. Buddhist Proverb

As the Pop More Corks clock reached 7:00 PM, once again it was time to close and lock the doors. Key in hand, I thought my evening mantra.

As I close this door, I am thankful for all the wonderful people and experiences that have been brought to me this day.

18

"I'D LIKE TO OPEN UP A WINE STORE"

Choosing a career often represents a difficult balance between earning a good income and cultivating your gifts. At any given time, there are certain professions that carry an aura of glamour in our society. There have always been the standbys like becoming a doctor or lawyer, but today working in banking and finance, with the chance to earn millions, carries a certain mystique. Then, there are the careers that are glamorous because they are connected to a certain cultural phenomenon.

John had been in to visit Pop More Corks on several occasions before sharing what his dream profession would be.

"I've been thinking about opening up a wine store. What do you think?" John asked.

"Before I answer that, tell me about what you're doing now," I inquired.

"I can't complain. I make good money remodeling Starbucks locations, but it just isn't enough anymore," John shared.

"When Starbucks sells a cup of coffee, how much of a dollar do they get to keep?" I asked.

"I really don't know, I just do the remodeling," John answered with a puzzled look on his face.

"I'm sure they operate on a high margin. I would guess that out of every dollar in the till, they keep 75 cents," I suggested.

"The potential for profit is built in to the product, isn't it? I'm thinking it's the same in the wine business," John added.

"I wish it were. When I take in a dollar, I only keep about 25 cents. The only reason this business works for me is because I'm not here to make a lot of money," I admitted.

"I'm surprised to hear that. I just assumed it would be a good business to get into because of the intense interest in wine in our society," John said, looking down sadly as if one of his lifelong dreams had just been shattered.

"I don't mean to discourage you, but that's the retail reality of the wine business. On the other hand, if wine is something you are passionate about, by all means, keep looking into the idea," I advised.

"I will . . . I will," John agreed before leaving.

*P*arable *R*eflections

Although a number of influences brought me to a place in my life where money clearly wasn't everything, getting there was a process. Working to rebuild my life after the stroke, I began to sense a greater Purpose building—that I would not go back to evaluating my work based on income alone.

Donny Deutsch, host of THE BIG IDEA, on CNBC, took a family business to the billion dollar mark before selling it and reinventing his life and his professional purpose. Money was no longer the measure. Today, he motivates many to identify their passion and when that moment of clarity presents itself, take that passion-driven idea and turn it into big profits.

Although the stated goal in his BIG IDEA headline is to make millions, he would be the first one to admit that the process is even more important. What provides human beings with the most satisfaction is to invest their creativity, their ability to do something they are passionate about and come up with some completely unique product or service, or a new approach to a product or service, and turn it into a thriving business.

Once you have taken that step, you are already a success. So often the big profits he talks about actually follow in time, but the fundamental satisfaction, the motivation, the joy of following your "bliss" into a professional endeavor is most important.

19

SHARING OPENS THE SOUL

As I open this door, may I be open to allowing all possibilities to be brought to me. I ask to be receptive to whatever and whoever comes my way this glorious day.

One day a couple wandered through the Pop More Cork's doors.

"Thanks for stopping in today. What brings you to Lake Geneva?"

"Oh, we're here to see our daughter who's living in the area," Mr. Johnson volunteered.

"What can you tell me about the art on your wall?" Mrs. Johnson questioned.

"Actually, my grandmother is the artist. I'm pleased you noticed them," I responded.

"I'm an artist myself and like to work in watercolors. I've done some similar scenes on canvas at home," she added.

The original art showcased on the Pop More Cork's walls is there for a reason. They remind me of my roots—where I came from and by association, the art reflects what is really important. Although I didn't grow up on the family farm, it was my family legacy, tended by my grandparents and father. Their way of life, lived in rural Wisconsin close to the land and connected to the cycle of life, has all but disappeared in our modern world.

In the world of wine production, there are also small family-owned wineries where a dedicated individual will nurture a small plot of land, growing, harvesting, and fermenting grapes into wines with character. Like the small rural Wisconsin farmer, owners who love what they do, who have responded to a calling, whose livelihood and happiness come from their passion for wine, are the human story behind the labels of the wine bottles found on the Pop More Corks shelves.

The trend toward homogenous, uniform mass production of so many of the goods and services in our modern global marketplace is disturbing and works against honoring diversity and recognizing the special gifts and place of the individual. The mass die-off of the family farm in America and throughout the world is a symptom of this trend. My father left the family farm, seduced by the opportunities of a more modern way of life in an urban area.

My aunt, on the other hand, married a small farm owner who was born on the kitchen table of their modest farm house, was raised, worked his entire life there, and died on that small dairy farm. Among the animals on the farm were a group of Alpacas, raised for their wool.

Every spring, my grandmother would shear the wool from the Alpacas, have it cleaned and carded, then, hand spin the wool into yarn. Since each Alpaca was genetically unique, their wool coloring was unique with blends ranging from black to white and many colors in between. That made her yarn unique in all the world. Like the grapes grown in a specific region of the world, the Alpacas roamed and grazed on the pasture of a unique plot of land during unique climate conditions affecting the color and texture of the wool resulting in a distinctly unique animal.

When artisans knit sweaters from the Alpaca yarn they often honor the animals that provided the wool by sewing in their individual names on the label. I keep samples of her yarns in Pop More Corks and show them to patrons as a way to share the story of my family farm heritage which flows into the value of the unique wines I promote explaining the source of their special character and what it represents in a broader sense.

As another disturbing sign of our times, unbelievably, after being shown the yarn, some people actually asked what yarn was used for! Sweaters do not grow on the shelves at Wal-Mart. Cheese does not sprout from a pool of cultured milk wrapped in cellophane.

Pop More Corks offers a selection of unique cheeses. One in particular is made from sheep's milk. More than that, it is a cheese made from the milk of one particular type called a Latxa sheep. Idiazabal cheese, to be called that, by law must be made from milk from Latxa sheep which graze in the pastures of the Basque region of Spain.

The cheese has an earthy, sharp, nutty flavor with a smooth texture. Such requirements guarantee the unique characteristics of a cheese with this name. Similarly, the wool from a particular Alpaca raised on a particular plot of land is unique, as is a wine fermented from a particular grove of grapes grown on the land in a particular region of the world.

How sad that we have become so far removed from the source of the gifts of nature that sustain our lives. Being detached from the source, we are no longer in control of the quality and character of the food we eat or the clothes we buy. For too many, most of what they buy has been manufactured by the millions in a homogenized manner. As such, it is not natural in the sense that it does not come directly from nature. It has been forced into a state of uniformity, when the heritage of anything that comes directly from nature is to be unique.

We need to honor diversity, for our value as human beings rests in the fact that each one of us is completely unique in all the world. From this diversity comes the creativity to adapt to change and this basic biological principal supports the forward progress of all life on earth.

On a sociological level, without preserving the value of diversity we risk losing the desire to explore the rich complexity of our world. If we, as a race, stop wanting to live and discover all the many distinct possibilities that life has to offer, our ability to keep evolving will be crippled. Today's youth are being affected by this problem.

Our children are bored with little to get excited about. They are mesmerized by the millions sitting in front of uniformly designed video games. They are corralled into herds of uniformly thinking and behaving sub humans by the power of mass media and culturally driven stereotypes. They can't get excited about eating a slice of Velveeta Cheese and unfortunately, their entire world has become homogenized.

On a less dramatic level, diversity in the things we consume can result in wonderfully complex and compelling tastes. Take, for example, a wine from Italy, from Tuscany, from the region in Tuscany called Carmignano. It is made from Sangiovese grapes and will taste like no other wine in the world.

Unfortunately, much of the world's wine is mass produced. Although I did not grow up on my family's farm, my roots are there and I honor those roots in my selection of Pop More Corks wines, created with the character that can only come from small regional producers.

After an extended conversation and tasting, The Johnson's left with two bottles of wine. A week later, a letter came in the Pop More Corks mailbox.

Dear David,

We just wanted to tell you how much we enjoyed our visit to Pop More Corks. The wine you recommended was outstanding and we wanted to thank you for spending so much time with us. If you're ever in Oshkosh, Wisconsin, do look us up so that we might return your courtesy and kindness.

Sincerely,
The Johnson's

A year later, the Johnson's returned to Pop More Corks. The store was busy and I didn't have much time to spend with them, but they waited, browsed, and weren't about to leave without saying hello and purchasing a bottle of wine.

I could tell they weren't really wine connoisseurs, nor did they have much discretionary income to spend on wine, but they did value the opportunity to communicate and share on a deeper level.

The sharing evolves naturally from the passion that fuels my deep interest in wine and from the comfort level that comes with a an extensive knowledge of wine. There is a values system that comes with my appreciation for the unique character of the special wines on the Pop More Corks shelves. After my stroke, a spiritual values system became a sustaining influence in my life.

Just as I am spontaneous in sharing my passion for wine and confident in sharing information about wine, I feel the same inspiration to share spiritual truths as I understand them when I feel someone might benefit from that sharing.

Don't be afraid to share your passionate interests with others. By doing so, you activate the revolving door of opportunity for them to open up to you. The result is the kind of indepth discourse that makes conversation stimulating and relevant. Everyone has something they are passionate about.

If you aren't fortunate enough to be earning a living through your passionate interest, cultivate that interest as a hobby and work toward transforming your hobby into a profession. Regardless, don't hesitate to share the important things in your life with others and grow on the feedback.

*P*arable *R*eflections

As we all work toward contributing to the Greater Good, the kind of Energy that will get us there as a world community is for each of us to be following their "bliss" as declared by Joseph Campbell, in his groundbreaking book, *The Power of Myth.* Engineered in that concept is the best that each of us has to offer toward achieving Peace on Earth through sharing our individual passions, followed by sharing our resources.

Currently there is so much discontent and confrontation and misunderstanding in the world. That destructive dynamic in our global society results from the fact that too many people are not grounded and satisfied by what they're doing to earn a living, often because they lead a daily struggle for subsistence and survival. To have the opportunities the rest of us take for granted, the world's resources must be reallocated, meaning those with much must learn to live a simpler life with less so that all might thrive.

Today's world is at a crossroads. We need many voices sharing the messages that will lead us all in the right direction and bring us together.

Many return to Pop More Corks as much for the open, empathetic, honest sharing as for the wines and wine tasting—and I am there as much for the opportunity to engage in a meaningful conversation as to run a business. Customers share of themselves with me—I share with them—and together we share a glass of fine Pop More Corks wine!

As the Pop More Corks clock reached 7:00 PM, once again it was time to close and lock the doors. Key in hand, I thought my evening mantra.

As I close this door, I am thankful for all the wonderful people and experiences that have been brought to me this day.

20

THE INEVITABLE CYCLE OF LIFE

As I open this door, may I be open to allowing all possibilities to be brought to me. I ask to be receptive to whatever and whoever comes my way this glorious day.

"I'm looking for a 2005 Ariel Cabernet Sauvingon. I've heard Ariel produces the highest quality non-alcoholic wine to be had. Would you agree?" Claire asked after looking through the Pop More Corks shelves and not finding any.

"I don't carry any non-alcoholic wine, but would you mind telling me why you need the wine to be free of alcohol?" I inquired, sensing that her request was about much more than finding a bottle of wine.

"I've got a lot going on right now . . . you know, life's little challenges, and I need to stay focused," Claire replied, without going into any detail about what was troubling her.

"Well, I can understand that, but consider this, when the alcohol is removed from a wine, much of the magic and complexity that gives the wine its character is extracted along with the alcohol," I added.

"Fortunately, I'm on the other side of a period in my life when I enjoyed my wine a little too much. I'm afraid to go back to those days," Clair decided to share.

"Well, many of us have been there and I respect your decision, but what did you mean when you mentioned dealing with life's little challenges?"

"Oh . . . just the usual, some family health and financial problems, but nothing I shouldn't be able to handle . . . I just need to stay sharp, especially right now," she said.

"I'm sorry to hear that, but I think I know how you must be feeling. Just the other day I slipped on some ice right outside my front door, slammed my head into the concrete and thought I had a concussion for sure," I shared.

"Oh, my, are you all right?"

"I had some troubling symptoms for a few days, but I'm definitely getting better."

"My mother took a nasty fall yesterday and is recovering at Saint Luke's in Woodstock. It was a close call and I was told it might be months before she is fully recovered, if she does recover," Clair said.

"You didn't mention if she broke her hip."

"No, fortunately she didn't, but it is fractured, she hurt her back, and there is something wrong with her hearing. The problem is that she lives with my father who is in his late 80s and he's not really able to take care of her. This is the first time in all my years that I've had to worry about them. They are very independent, always have been, they love their home, and it won't be easy to get them to leave under any circumstances. I know the day is coming when they won't be able to live there alone, but the subject just hasn't come up and isn't likely to. My father just isn't the type to talk about anything of real substance, I'm afraid."

"That is difficult. I went through something similar when my mother became ill. There were months of convalescing, then, after she passed I ended up moving my father to Wisconsin to be near our family members."

"That must have been a challenging period for you," Clair said.

"Yes, it was, but like most problems in life, you cope the best you can and try to keep moving forward. You mentioned some financial problems," I brought up.

"Well, nothing that serious, but my father called the other day all worried about his dwindling assets. I'm not really sure if he is having real problems or if he's just getting paranoid about money. I know his mother died at 96 in a nursing home and I'm sure he worries about that happening to him."

"That is something you'll have to check in to," I suggested.

"For example, the doctor wanted my mother to get a walker and my father wasn't sure if Medicare would pay or if they had the money to just go out and buy it. Little things like that, but if they are struggling with money, again, it's the first time my husband and I will have to begin diverting our resources to begin to cover their expenses," Claire revealed.

"Have you set up or would you want to have power of attorney documents in place to make medical and financial decisions for your parents?" I inquired.

"You know, my dad may be old, but his mind is sharp and he handles all their finances to this day and has all his life. It would not be easy to suggest that he give up that function, and besides, I can see it is good for him."

"And I suppose you have children you're still responsible for as well?" I asked.

"Yes we do; a teenager still at home and his older brother away at college. I suppose another reason I'm feeling stretched is that my younger son arranged for an AFS student to stay with us and he'll be here until June."

"Well, you're certainly performing a wonderful service being part of the foreign exchange program for students. It is undoubtedly a sacrifice, but what better way to build bridges of compassion and understanding among the peoples and cultures of our troubled world," I replied.

"I can appreciate those sentiments as a broad concept, and I know I shouldn't feel this way, but I was just getting used to having more freedom and privacy after my oldest left for college, and now, Demetri, he's from Russia, is always around. He's an early riser like I am and the time I used to have to myself, early in the morning before the rest of the family got up, I now have to share with him. Just little things, really, but together they're taking a toll."

"I can see why, and you have every reason to feel that way," I empathetically suggested.

"So, now you see why I came in looking for a bottle of wine? If things don't get better soon, I may have to rethink my preference for Ariel wines!" she quipped.

Claire's mother was being treated in the same hospital where I got medical care first for my stroke, then, for my hip replacement. I knew that substantial recovery, even from a serious health crisis, was possible.

"Well, I wish I could be more helpful."

"Like I said before, this is something lots of other people are going through and I'm sure we'll get through it as well. Right now I just want to take it one week at a time, get through the holidays, and deal with the problems one at a time as they come up. You know, thank you for listening. I just realized how much it helps to get things in perspective if you can just talk about them. Thank you." Claire said before leaving.

*P*arable *R*eflections

When you're young it seems as if your life will stretch on into eternity. With experience, we begin to get glimpses of our mortality. Allow those insights to lead you to an understanding and respect for the importance of the cycle of life and our place in that great cycle.

Instead of fearing death, embrace the transitional role death plays in the renewal of life and in establishing reference points around which we define our existence.

As the Pop More Corks clock reached 7:00 PM, once again it was time to close and lock the doors. Key in hand, I thought my evening mantra.

As I close this door, I am thankful for all the wonderful people and experiences that have been brought to me this day.

21

SAVING THE HIBISCADELPHUS WOODII

As I open this door, may I be open to allowing all possibilities to be brought to me. I ask to be receptive to whatever and whoever comes my way this glorious day.

"I saw your wine tasting sign. I'm interested in your recommendation for a wine to serve with a Hawaiian dinner I'm planning for some friends over the weekend," Helen opened boldly after walking into Pop More Corks on a bitterly cold winter day between Christmas and New Year's.

"Welcome, and I believe your request is a first for a Pop More Corks customer! Please tell me more. What are you serving and what is your connection to Hawaii, the island and prime winter tourist destination?" I inquired, knowing there might be an interesting story behind her opening request.

"Actually, I recently returned after a year-long tour working for the conservation agency there," Helen comfortably volunteered.

"Well, that explains your putting on a Hawaiian dinner for your friends, and it also tells me you had fond memories of your experiences there," I suggested.

"I certainly did, and it was not easy to leave," Helen added.

"What were you doing?"

"I'm a plant ecologist working for the Hawaiian Biological Survey. A number of native Hawaiian species, over 200 actually, are endangered from the competition of introduced species. Even our state flower, the Hibiscus brachenridgei, is endangered. If you've ever been there, you know what a paradise the Hawaiian Islands are. It is a challenge for the government to protect the land from excessive commercial development and from the unanticipated effects of visitors from foreign lands introducing plant species that did not evolve with the native plants," Helen explained at some length.

"I can see that not only are you well trained, but your tone suggests a passion for this issue and your role in trying to make a difference for good in Hawaii," I said.

"Too often our team is fighting a losing battle, but it's important that someone take up the standard to protect endangered species, don't you agree?" Helen declared with the fervor of a dedicated advocate for the cause.

"I certainly do. I've only been there through the pages of National Geographic, but from what I've seen, the pristine conditions are well worth preserving, no matter the cost. In my own way, I'm holding up the same standard in support of diversity through my selection of wines. To get back to your original question, what will you be serving at your dinner?" I asked.

"I'm planning on a blackened mahi-mahi fillet for the main course, along with a fruit salad mix of pineapple, papaya, star fruit, avocado, banana, mango and macadamia nuts, and some steamed greens, ginger shavings, and okra on the plate, but please tell me more about your diverse wine selection?" Helen requested, always eager to engage someone who shares her belief in the importance of preserving nature's rich biological diversity.

"Before I suggest a wine for the meal you're planning, tell me more about your conservation work."

"In general, as I mentioned earlier, we're focused on any endangered plant species, but most of our attention was dedicated to a plant that has declined to the point where we can find only one example living in the wild on the side of a cliff, the Hibiscadelphus woodii. Unfortunately, at that point the species becomes what we refer to as genetically extinct because there aren't enough thriving members to make seeds while continuing to refresh the DNA from generation to generation."

"Is there anything you can do in that case?"

"Well, it's something like what was done to restore the Condor population in California by hand rearing hatchlings from harvested eggs. Without damaging the one thriving plant, we can harvest the seeds and grow individual plants in the lab for reintroduction in the wild. This, of course, is not easy given the plant's location. Members of our team have to rappel down the steep cliff using mountaineering gear and climbing techniques. It's dangerous and we've had some success with this strategy, but there are no guarantees and this is only one of about a dozen other plants we're working to preserve."

"My compliments on your efforts! Of course, not only plant species, but animals on land and in the sea are at risk from man's influences like global warming and widespread pollution. Like I said, I'm fighting a similar battle to preserve the dignity and value of the smaller independent wineries around the world who have not sold out to the big companies engineering diversity out of their wines produced for a mass consumption market," I explained, supporting Helen's passion for the subject in my remarks.

"So, are you ever going to answer my original question and suggest a wine for my dinner? This is not just a dinner. I'll be serving up a healthy portion of reasons to support this cause with my family who'll be attending, so I need everything to be as perfect as possible," Helen added.

"Ok, I'm ready. Step over to the wine tasting counter and let's pick out just the right wine for the occasion. Did you say you were serving a blackened fish?"

"Yes, seared blackened mahi-mahi."

"Anytime you're serving food with a spicy accent you need a fruity wine. You don't want a wine that is overly oaked, or that has tannins from oak, or a too dry red wine with a tannic feel, because those flavors will directly clash with the spices in the blackened fish. Mahi-mahi is a flavorful fish. You could choose a red or white wine, but I'd recommend a white."

"That works for me."

"Great, let's taste a wine from Alsace with a blend of Pinot Blanc, a little bit of Gewurztraminer, and a touch of Riesling. The Pinot Blanc is going to make it nice and crisp, clean and refreshing, and it will be able to cut through the oily aspect of the fish while the Gewurztraminer will add a floral note with the Riesling providing a fruit-forward character.

It's still going to be a dry wine with some nice soft fruit to it which will compliment the flavors in the meal you're serving. This particular wine, Hugel Gentil, is a uniquely blended proprietary wine only created by this small producer representing their house style. You won't find this wine from anyone else in that area, or from anyone else anywhere.

"It's made to bear the pure flavor character fingerprint of their house, not confused by any oak aging . . . and reflect the pure flavors of the fruit grown in the Alsace in France. This wine is uniquely expressing the style of what Pinot Blanc grown in Alsace can taste like, blended with just a little bit of Riesling, and a little bit of Gewurztraminer. Each grape embodies the effects of cool climate, unique soil . . . one of a kind . . . not unlike that rare plant you're trying so hard to preserve.

"It is not expensive, yet it is a high quality wine that would be a wonderful complement to your dinner, and its history can contribute to the dinner conversation you're planning to go along with the blackened mahi-mahi!" I suggested, being fully aware of her intention to raise the issue of the fundamental importance of her work preserving diversity with her family.

Helen has been on several tours of duty in Hawaii and makes a point to return to Pop More Corks each time she is back home. Over the months, I've met Helen's sister and father. Helen is from an affluent family who can't always understand why she would dedicate her life to the cause of preserving endangered plant species.

*P*arable *R*eflections

Each of us, in our own way, can work to promote the important, but not always popular value of preserving diversity in nature, sensing, if not sure, that the destiny of every species, including man, rests in a world where all living beings are valued equally for their role in maintaining the delicate cycle and balance of living systems on our precious planet Earth.

As the Pop More Corks clock reached 7:00 PM, once again it was time to close and lock the doors. Key in hand, I thought my evening mantra.

As I close this door, I am thankful for all the wonderful people and experiences that have been brought to me this day.

22

NIGERIA – A MIRROR ON OUR TROUBLED WORLD

As I open this door, may I be open to allowing all possibilities to be brought to me. I ask to be receptive to whatever and whoever comes my way this glorious day.

"Are we in the right place for the wine tasting? We saw the sign outside," Mathew inquired while paused at the front door.

"Yes you are, and be sure and bring in your friend," I replied, after noticing that Mathew's companion seemed a bit shy about walking through the Pop More Corks door.

"David, I'd like you to meet my friend, Ronald, who is visiting from Nigeria," Mathew began.

"Hello, Ronald. So pleased to meet you and welcome to Pop More Corks. What brings you half way around the world to Lake Geneva, Wisconsin?" I inquired, always delighted to take a vicarious trip to a new land through the eyes and experience of one of my customers.

"I work at the American Consulate in the capital city, Abuja. Most of us are Americans and the team understands the importance of getting back home often enough to keep our sanity. As you can imagine, conditions are not good in Nigeria or in most of the countries on the African continent, but enough about that for now. I was looking forward to tasting some red wines. I need to pick a good one to bring to a dinner party I've been invited to," Ronald shared.

"I can help you there. I have four wines open, all made from the Pinot Noir grape varietal," were my opening remarks.

"I haven't heard that term before. What does *varietal* mean?" Matthew asked.

"Think of apples. Years ago there were only a handful of apple varieties available in stores. Today, there are many more. It's the same with grapes. Pinot Noir is a type of grape, as is Cabernet Sauvignon. In the world of wine, different grapes are referred to as varietals. Like apples, think about tasting a Gala, a Fuji, and a Golden Delicious, uniquely different flavors come to mind based on those different varieties of apples. If you go out into a vineyard and taste three different varietals of grapes, like the apples you will be able to taste the differences, and because they taste differently, they will ferment into uniquely different wines. The grape varietal, and where the grapes are grown, are the two main factors controlling the taste of wine. Even two Pinot Noir grapes grown in different parts of the world will ferment into discernibly different wines. So, today we're going to taste four red wines made from the same type of grape, Pinot Noir, but grown in different regions."

"What, then, accounts for the differences that can be significant from year to year?" Ronald wondered.

"During each growing season the vines are subjected to a unique climate with varying amounts of rain, sun, and warmth, all of which can affect the quality of the grape. That being the case, I believe that a good wine maker can produce a quality wine from year to year no matter the fluctuations in climate. It won't be the same, it won't taste the same, but it can be a good wine. This first wine, a Jean Garaudet Hautes-Cotes de Beaune is a Pinot Noir from France, from the region of France called Burgundy, and from the area in Burgundy called Cote de Beaune. Within this legally defined area, if you are making red wine and using the place name, by law only Pinot Noir grapes can be used. As you taste this wine, you'll notice, like all Pinot Noirs, it is lighter-bodied with a Bing cherry flavor, certainly not as heavy as a big full-bodied Cabernet Sauvignon. And so, it is expressing the Pinot Noir characteristics, but because it is from France, where it is cooler, it will also express a layered, earthy, almost mushroom quality. It's much less about the big, rich, ripe fruit that we're going to experience from the other wines, and more about the layers of earthy characteristics, more typical of cool climate Pinot Noirs. During tastings, it is best to begin with lighter, dryer Old World wines and move to the richer, typically more full-bodied New World wines."

"I do like this, although it is dry," Matthew decided.

"This wine, with its earthy characteristics would match up well with a nice filet smothered in sautéed mushrooms," I added.

"Our second wine, today, Te Kairanga, comes from New Zealand, from the Marlborough region. Usually Sauvignon Blanc is thought of as the premier wine exported from New Zealand, but over the past four or five years, they've become known for producing excellent Pinot Noir wines. Located deep in the southern hemisphere, their consistently cool climate is one of the main reasons because the Pinot Noir grape varietal thrives in cool environments. Some people think the Pinot Noir's of New Zealand are very close in style to the wines from Burgundy, in France. A New Zealand Pinot Noir has a bit more fruit to it and a really nice bright acidity that jumps out at you. This Te Kairanga shares layers of earth and spice with the Burgundy Pinot Noir and would go well with a fresh grilled salmon fillet. Salmon is a richer textured, somewhat oily fish, as compared to a pike or a whitefish, and it can take a wine with more weight and body. Even though you often think of white wine with fish, a type with more body, like salmon, can go well with a lighter style red, like this Te Kairanga Pinot Noir from the Marlborough in New Zealand. Next, we're going to travel across the Pacific Ocean, east to Oregon."

"I've never thought of Oregon as being a wine producing area," Ronald said.

"For exceptional Pinot Noir, as of the last twenty years Oregon is one of the regions in the world people think of first. This next wine is a Ponzi Willamette Valley Pinot Noir. The Burgundy, in France, is where the grape variety got its origin. From there, it was brought to California, where they focused on finding the cooler areas. When the wine industry got started in Oregon, about 25-30 years ago, and because Oregon is on the same latitude as Burgundy, with a similar climate, it was thought, and correctly so, that the Pinot Noir grape would thrive there. This particular Pinot

Noir comes from vineyards carefully managed using sustainable, ecologically sound, agriculture principles. Dick Ponzi, who owns this winery, was one of the pioneers successfully growing Pinot Noir in Oregon. As compared to the New Zealand Pinot Noir, this wine is a shade darker and a step up in weight and richness, with more body, complexity, and also features those Bing cherry flavors. Think about what it's like to bite into a firm, plump, ripe Bing cherry. You get that rush of cherry juice, but when you get right next to the pit, the flavor turns a touch bitter. When I taste a good Pinot Noir, I react to a little bitterness from the tannins in the wine while sensing the right balance between the sweet fruit flavors and the tannic edge. This Ponzi Pinot Noir expresses the classic Oregon style of Pinot Noir. Next, we're headed down to the central coast of California, to an area where it is substantially warmer.

"Because of the warmer climate, the grapes are going to ripen more thoroughly and the riper the grapes get, the more the wine will present an intense fruit flavor with more weight, body, and richness. This Santa Rita Hills Pinot Noir is produced just outside of Santa Barbara, and is becoming well known for the quality of their Pinot Noir. As compared to the regions where the first three wines were produced, this area is substantially warmer with a longer growing season for the grapes and therefore this Pinot Noir presents with the bigger, richer flavors, almost heading in the direction of a Cabernet with respect to the weight and body of the wine. Some Pinot Noir purists who prefer the French style, with a lighter, more focused earthy character, would say that this is not a classic style of Pinot Noir."

"After tasting these wines, I can see that everything you said about the growing region making a dramatic difference is certainly true," Ronald confirmed after swirling, then swallowing, the last sample in his glass.

"It's not up to me to say that one is better than the others, but as you can see, they are all unique and they all fit and serve different purposes."

"What can you tell me about how this global warming problem is affecting wineries around the world?" Ronald asked.

"I've heard that the California wineries, for example, are planning to compensate for the increasing temperatures. I don't know if or when that will happen, but generally speaking, grape varietals will not be able to adapt quickly to warmer conditions and so the wineries will be forced to relocate their vineyards to more northern climates if the warming trend intensifies. More likely, rather than moving, the producers will change the grape variety they grow to those more suited for the climate conditions in their vineyards. I'm sure the industry will work at developing new varietals better suited to changing temperature patterns. For example, Cabernet Sauvignon grapes require a long growing season and a warm climate in order to ripen which is why they are grown in the Napa Valley. So there are natural differences already in the many grape varieties used by the wine industry. That's not to say that the potential problems associated with unchecked global warming are minor. The kinds of climate changes we're seeing normally take thousands of years to slowly change during natural climate cycles, but, of course, we're forcing rapid change through the greenhouse gasses we're pumping into the atmosphere."

"Perhaps it will take something dramatic, like California no longer able to grow grapes, that will shock people into finally doing something about global warming," Ronald suggested.

"How is the climate in your country? I know a little bit about the topography of Nigeria with the southern half being tropical rainforest, then transitioning to desert conditions to the north," I said.

"Drought and famine are all too common throughout Africa and the unstable world climate seems to be a factor in Africa and in Nigeria with desertification on the rise, but nobody knows for sure," Ronald replied.

"What is currently going on with the politics and economy of Nigeria?" I asked.

"Nigeria is unexpectedly diverse culturally and in terms of religious orientation with over 200 ethnic groups inhabiting their 36 states. About half the country is Christian, half Muslim, so you can imagine the related problems in terms of governing two such groups that can't seem to get along anywhere in the world, much less within a single country where they must live side by side," Ronald added.

"Isn't Nigeria a member of OPEC?" I asked.

"Yes, since the 70's, and you'd think the oil revenue would have solved all their social and political problems, but that's not what happened," Ronald shared.

"I imagine the usual graft took over and only a relatively few shared in the financial windfall."

"That's about it. The military prospered and democracy suffered, but there is a democratically elected president right now and things are moving in the right direction. Oil revenue is slowly reaching the people. Of course, our job at the consulate is to make sure the oil keeps flowing to the global market at reasonable prices which also means holding down the political turmoil in the country," Ronald explained.

"Well, Ronald, you're living an aspect of a personal dream I've always had, to travel and see the world, but for now, I'm content that good people like you, from all over the world, come here to visit me," I shared with just a tinge of jealousy.

*P*arable *R*eflections

Once again, my intention to be open to sharing with anyone who was moved to walk through the Pop More Corks doors was honored. On this day, the problems of the small country, Nigeria, were empathetically reviewed by two people who understood the greater Truth that poverty, illness, and injustice in one place on Earth is a real problem for everyone, everywhere.

Can struggling countries like Nigeria join the global community of thriving nations without being absorbed by them? Such countries can and must be helped while still honoring their national integrity, their right to exist, and their cultural and religious diversity.

Karmic forces will continue to impact the world leading to wars, illness, poverty, and even conditions like global warming, unless the world joins together to bring peace and prosperity to all through sharing our resources with those in need.

As the Pop More Corks clock reached 7:00 PM, once again it was time to close and lock the doors. Key in hand, I thought my evening mantra.

As I close this door, I am thankful for all the wonderful people and experiences that have been brought to me this day.

23

KEEP MOVING FORWARD

As I open this door, may I be open to allowing all possibilities to be brought to me. I ask to be receptive to whatever and whoever comes my way this glorious day.

Luanne, a thirty-something attractive single female, walked into Pop More Corks looking for a new wine to add to her enjoyment of a DVD she was planning to watch at home that evening. As we talked, I could tell that she often paused so as to reflect on what was just said, or to process the content of what was said to her for just a moment, before going on with the conversation. I noticed her dog fussing outside while tied to a bike rack.

"I can see you're worried about your dog. Do bring him in, it's all right," I suggested.

"Are you sure you don't mind? I hate to leave him alone," Luanne replied.

"Not at all."

I went to get the bowl and treats I keep handy for just such occasions. It took me a few minutes and Luanne couldn't help but notice me struggling with my movement. When I returned to the counter, she asked me a question.

"David, have you had a stroke or something?"

"It's been a while now . . . over ten years, but, yes, I did."

"Well, I don't know if you could tell, but so have I," Luanne shared, almost relieved to meet someone who might actually understand what she'd been through during the past months of post-stroke recovery.

"I did notice you taking some time to process what I said to you, but that was all and I really didn't suspect you'd had a stroke. What exactly happened and what has your recovery been like?" I asked.

"For me, it all began with a virus I couldn't shake. That led to kidney failure and soon after a kidney transplant, I suffered a stroke, which is not that uncommon, but it happened to me and really complicated my recovery," Luanne explained.

"You've been through quite a struggle to regain your health, but you seem pretty well to me right now. Are there any functions you haven't recovered yet?" I asked.

"My conversation skills are almost back to normal, but something happened that makes it almost impossible for me to read and despite therapy, that hasn't improved in months. Writing is very difficult for me as well."

"How about testing your conversation skills during a wine tasting?"

"That would be outstanding. I promised myself I'd bring home an interesting red wine to watch with a film tonight."

"I can help you with that. We'll be tasting four red wines today."

"Is there a right or wrong way to do this?" Luanne asked, never having formally tasted wines before.

"First of all just swirl the wine in the glass and smell the aromas, then, take a small sip, allowing the wine to roll around on your tongue. You should sense different flavors on different parts of your tongue. As you swallow, notice if the flavors hang on or disappear right away. Try to identify the flavors that presented on the different parts of your tongue—tip, back, and sides," I explained.

"That sounds like a tall order, but I'll do my best!"

"This first wine is a Fitou from France, from the Languedoc region of far southern

France. In the Languedoc is a small town named, Fitou. In and around Fitou may be as many as 100 different vineyards. To be called a Fitou, first the grapes must come from the vineyards surrounding the town and be blended with at least 40% of the Carignan grape varietal. This is a special Fitou. If you take a look at the label, you'll see twelve names on the front, and twelve pictures on the back. The 100 or so vineyards are owned and operated by small farmers who don't have the resources to operate their own wineries, but each year they take their grapes to a co-op winery. For this particular Fitou, the grapes from all the vineyards were judged for quality and the top twelve from the year 2005 went into the blend for this wine with their names and pictures placed on the label. It is considered the best of the Fitou wines produced in that year. This Les Douze Fitou has 60% Carignan blended with Grenache and Syrah grapes. Like so many of my wines, this Fitou is in limited production, sending only a few thousand cases to the States each year. It's a medium bodied style red wine with a nice dark berry fruit character and an earthy edge, but not as fruit-forward as one of the wines we're going to taste later on."

"Would you recommend this wine with a meal?" Luanne wondered?

"Certainly, with its characteristics, I can see serving this Fitou with a hearty beef stew or any meal with a rich sauce foundation," I suggested.

"It has a really good first flavor to it, but a little earthy for my taste and the alcohol is strong, there at the end. Yes, that does fill the mouth, and it lasts on the tongue. "What else do you have?" Luanne asked.

"This next wine, Luzon de Luzon, is from the Jumilla in Spain, and made of two grape varietals, 75% Monastrell and 25% Syrah. The Jumilla region is hilly, bordering on mountainous, and the vineyards are up about 1,000 feet, with relatively thin soils. Because of these conditions, the grapes don't get overly ripe. Because of the Monastrell, or Mourvedre, both names referring to the same type of grape by the way, the wine will have a rustic, earthy edge to it. The Syrah brings a nice, dark, blackberry fruit character to the wine. It has some good backbone, but it's not as overwhelmingly fruit-forward as the Australian red. That's right, you're not that fond of a wine with earthy flavors, are you?"

"Not always, depends on the wine, and this is OK, but I'm not sure," Luanne admitted.

"Will you be having the wine with food tonight?" I asked.

"No, probably not."

"Just by itself?"

"I'd like the Luzon de Luzon with some spaghetti or lasagna. It seems like it would bring out the flavor of the sauce," Luanne decided.

"Yep, I agree. It is a wonderful straight forward wine that would go well with just about any simple meal. What you might not be liking is the alcohol finish," I suggested.

"I'm not always sure, but what I do know is that I love trying new things! What's next?" Luanne asked, with a delighted sense of anticipation beaming from her face.

"Moving on, we'll taste two different wines made from the same grape varietal, but because they come from different parts of the world, you will easily be able to tell them apart. The first wine, called Poitevin, comes from Bordeaux in France. In Bordeaux there is a small sub region, Medoc, on the left bank of the Gironde River estuary in Bordeaux. When you're in Bordeaux making wine, you can blend up to five different grape varietals, the main ones being Cabernet Sauvignon, Merlot, Cabernet Franc, Malbec, and Petite Verdot. Because this wine is coming from a region on the Left Bank, mainly Cabernet Sauvignon grapes will be used to make the wine, whereas, on the Right Bank mainly Merlot would be used in the blend. This Left Bank Bordeaux will be much different stylistically from the Australian Cabernet Sauvignon we will be tasting next. The difference you'll notice represents a classic comparison between a New World and Old World wine. The Old World wines are much more about linear layers of flavor expressed on the tongue from front to back, with earthy herbal tones and minerality, while the New World wines are more about side-to-side broad, mouth-filling, fruit-forward flavors. When you try the Cabernet Sauvignon from Australia, you'll see that it explodes with big, rich fruit and fills your mouth with flavor. So, here's some Poitevin from Bordeaux, Cabernet Sauvignon based with some Merlot and Cabernet Franc, and notice the more linear and front-to-back flavor profile. This wine goes well with food; a nice steak or some prime rib."

"The next wine we'll be tasting, a Nugan Cabernet Sauvignon from southeast Australia, is much more about that big, broad fruit-forward style featuring deep dark red fruit flavors such as black currant, blackberry, and plum, it has a classic, juicy, jammy Australian style. You should find it to be full bodied and fruit forward. This Nugan Cabernet is made from Cabernet Sauvignon grapes, and because they are grown in the warm climate of Australia, the wine has a broad, mouth-filling fruit character."

"There's no question about it. The differences and contrasts are obvious, even to my uneducated palate. Again, which one would you recommend as a sipping wine to enjoy without food?" Luanne confirmed, then asked.

"The Australian Cabernet Sauvignon is soft and lush for a Cabernet, without any bitter tannic edge, and would be a nice wine to drink as a cocktail," I suggested.

"About your conversations skills, I'd say you're doing well in that area, and about the reading, that's understandable . . . the two functions, speaking and reading, are related, I imagine. I struggled with some cognitive issues right after my stroke as well. I couldn't recognize certain patterns and make sense out of them. I forgot all my passwords, phone numbers, and that kind of thing and had to relearn everything," I added.

"I'm still working at it, but it's hard to make much progress," Luanne admitted.

"I can see you may be still hoping for a full recovery, and this may be hard for you to understand, but having a stroke was the best thing that ever happened to me," I shared, not at all intending to trivialize what Luanne had been through.

"That, you will have to explain to me!"

"I don't expect you or anyone to get this, but I wasn't in a good place in my professional life, in my personal life, in my heart, or soul when the stroke hit. It hasn't been easy, sacrifices were made, but for the first time I feel I'm in exactly the right place doing exactly what I was meant to do and I wouldn't go back to where I was before the stroke, even if I could," I attempted to explain.

"You know, I'm not quite that far along, but I can relate to what you're saying. Having a stroke has forced me to re-evaluate my entire life, all my goals, everything I used to think was so important. I'm still processing, but I'm glad we had a chance to talk because now I know that what happened to me needn't be all bad," Luanne attempted to explain.

"There is no doubt about it . . . much good can come from even the most awful tragedy. It's impossible to see that good in the beginning, but if you exercise your power to choose the good and focus on moving forward, the sun will rise on better days," were my encouraging words learned through my own experience working through personal tragedy.

"Just thinking about some of what's happened, I learned that my boyfriend really didn't love me. At first we moved here and began living together because he said he wanted to give me a kidney and eventually get married. Well, that didn't work out and he's out of my life now. I suppose it was a good thing that I found that out about him before we got married."

"There, you see . . . if you try, you can always find something worthwhile no matter what you're going through."

"I'm doing better now . . . I'm working and taking care of myself for the first time in my life. I think learning to be independent is something else I may never have accomplished if it weren't for the stroke," Luanne added reflectively.

"I wouldn't be here enjoying my new professional life running Pop More Corks, and meeting extraordinary people like you if it weren't for my stroke," I shared, meaning every word, despite the cost involved in the aftermath of post-stroke symptoms.

"I think I understand what you're trying to say."

*P*arable *R*eflections

In the journey through life, our fragile mortal bodies carry our souls through a process of learning and growing toward enlightenment. We are not here to live perfect, successful, long lives and die wealthy. Rather, our life experiences are often the key to learning, sometimes hard, but important lessons.

As the Pop More Corks clock reached 7:00 PM, once again it was time to close and lock the doors. Key in hand, I thought my evening mantra.

As I close this door, I am thankful for all the wonderful people and experiences that have been brought to me this day.

24

WHAT DOES IT PROFIT A MAN . . .

As I open this door, may I be open to allowing all possibilities to be brought to me. I ask to be receptive to whatever and whoever comes my way this glorious day.

Downtown Lake Geneva, like so many other small towns across America, thrives on the entrepreneurial spirit that fuels the successful small businesses providing the economic backbone for community residents. Becoming an accepted member of the relatively small family of store owners who keep the heart of downtown Lake Geneva thriving, is a difficult badge of honor to achieve. On a

Friday, the youngest member of the Lake Geneva Chamber of Commerce stepped through the Pop More Corks doors.

"Hello Jacob. I see you're finally open. I stopped in yesterday, but I didn't see you. How are things going?" I opened, always pleased to see one of my peer group of downtown business owners.

"So far so good, and you haven't seen me because I'm constantly on the go running errands. I've had to wear many hats to make ends meet. I don't have to tell you," Jacob shared before walking toward the wine tasting counter.

"Do I, and as you know, the work never ends, but it sure is worth it," I added.

"You're right about the work never ending, but right now I'm not so sure it is going to be worth it. I'm struggling to reorganize so as to find every penny of profit and reduce my overhead to the absolute minimum," Jacob was able to honestly share with someone he assumed was operating the same way.

"Don't be too hard on yourself. You've just gotten underway and it's going to take some time to sort everything out," I suggested.

"I spent so much time and money preparing for the opening, and some of my calculations I can see are off. I've really got to get back to the drawing board and restructure as soon as possible," he added.

"Just how detailed is your business profile?" I asked.

"I've got it worked out so I know exactly how much money I'm making for each hour of the day that I'm open, and I'm tracking the hourly expenses whenever I'm there or I have an employee with me."

"That is a lot of potentially valuable information to process. You should be able to make good use of it."

"So far I've learned that the evening hours lose money, so I'm planning to close sooner. That should help the bottom line right away," Jacob declared, pleased to have come up with a strategy to stop some of the red line bleeding right away.

"I can understand your concern about maximizing profits, but running a business in Lake Geneva isn't like day-trading stocks. You're part of a family here and I can tell you from experience, it takes time to get to know your family members, your customer base, and learn how to best serve them," I suggested, coming from my months of experience seeing my base of loyal customers grow steadily through word of mouth recommendations.

"I hear you, but I can't sleep at night if I think I'm not taking steps to cut my losses, yes, on an hourly basis, but that's me. I guess accounting is my thing . . . it always has been. I'm not sure why I took the risk to start my own business. I think I was happier when I was managing other people's money, but it's too late to turn back now. I've got to find a way to make this work," Jacob added revealing his deep fears about committing to a business that might end up failing.

"I can see you're upset, but give it time. You're a good businessman. Everything will work out. After all, we're in the middle of winter and although Lake Geneva is becoming more and more a year-round tourist destination, winters are going to be slow. If I were you, instead of worrying about cutting costs right now, I'd be planning on how to handle the crowds when the summer season hits!" I encouraged.

"Thanks David, I'll try to remember that and perhaps I'll start getting some sleep at night. Now, help me get my mind off of all this for a few minutes. Can we taste some wine?"

"Absolutely, and since you're clearly in need of a distraction, let's travel the globe during this wine tasting. For our first wine, we'll be going to Europe. Try this Prosecco," I suggested.

"That is good. Where does it come from?" Jacob asked.

"Our first stop is the Veneto in Italy. A tourist visiting there would almost certainly experience a delightful sparkling wine produced in the area, Prosecco. Made with the Champagne process, this Nino Franco Prosecco Rustico we're tasting, possesses a fruit-forward and slightly nutty character. If you were in Venice and visited the famous Harry's Wine Bar, you would be encouraged to try their signature drink, the Belini, a cocktail drink made in a flute. The recipe begins with a couple of ounces of white peach nectar, then, fill the flute up with our Prosecco, and finally it is often topped off with a drizzle of raspberry liquor to provide some extra fruit flavor—a great way to mark the day as festive and special, and it also goes well with breakfast or lunch. The base wine for this drink is our Prosecco which is also good by itself."

"Painting that picture makes this wine taste even better," Jacob admitted.

"From Italy, let's travel to South Africa, to an area known as Stellenbosch, one of the major grape growing regions in southern Africa. We're tasting a Ken Forester Petite Chenin Blanc made of 100% Chenin Blanc grapes. This grape variety is grown all over the world. If grown in the Loire Valley in France it would result in a sweeter, fruit-forward style of wine. When grown in California, the wine would be even sweeter, but in South Africa the grape ferments to a refreshing, clean style of white wine with crisp acidity and is often used as an aperitife with appetizers or as a cocktail by itself. This wine is fermented in stainless steel containers ensuring the flavors are not compromised with oak tannins. Now, let's cross the Atlantic heading for

America and the Russian River Valley in California."

"Taste this Buehler Russian River Valley Chardonnay," I suggested while pouring a sample into Jacob's glass.

"The grape variety in this wine is Chardonnay, and the region where the grapes are grown is the Russian River Valley in Sonoma County. This wine is both fermented and aged in oak barrels. In addition to the crisp apple flavors from the Chardonnay grapes, you'll be able to detect some vanilla and a spicy character. Those additional complexities come from the oak barrel aging. This wine happens to be made by John Buehler whose winery facilities are located in the Napa Valley, but he gets his grapes from the Russian River Valley. If you visit the Buehler winery you'll see an impressive statue of the Buddha. The owner of the Russian River Valley vineyards is a Buddhist. He used to sell his grapes to other wineries, but after establishing a relationship with John Buehler, he ships all his grapes to the Buehler winery for processing. The Russian River Valley Chardonnay you're tasting, is a great value at $11.99 a bottle as they often will go for upwards of $20 a bottle."

"Is that unusual for wineries to use grapes from other vineyards rather than grow their own?" Jacob asked.

"Not at all . . . it's common, actually," I replied.

"The next red wine is also from the Russian River Valley. This wine, Angeline, is made from Pinot Noir grapes and as you can see is a translucent ruby red. With light wines like this you might expect the flavor to be thin. This wine will surprise you with full classic Pinot Noir Bing cherry fruit character. Also fermented and aged in oak barrels, it has spicy vanilla and cinnamon nuances along with bright fruit flavors, making for a nice light to medium bodied red wine that would be marvelous with a pork tenderloin or grilled chicken breast. For our next wine, we're leaving America and heading back to Europe.

"This Spanish wine comes from the Tierra de Castilla, a large area encompassing the entire central region of Spain. The wine is made from a blend of two grape varietals, Tempranillo and Garnacha. Compared to the Pinot Noir, it certainly has more substance, more body, more weight, but it still isn't a full bodied wine. It is darker with more fruit flavors and has a rustic, earthy character with a very nice fruit-forward style. Retailing at $7.99, it is an exceptional value. I can guarantee any wine buyer that this modestly priced wine, compared to a commercially produced million-case California Cabernet Sauvingon, is brimming over with exceptional character and flavor."

"I don't understand why a producer with a quality wine would retail at such a low price,"

Jacob questioned, his accountant's mind instinctively stretching for profit potential.

"There are a number of factors involved in pricing wines. In Spain, the land where the grapes are grown is often much less valuable than, for example, in Napa Valley in California. Labor costs are lower in Spain. And then there is the producer's outlook. Any $7.99 wine from California will be retailed by huge corporate interests who have often times sacrificed character to maximize profits in their formulation of the wine. One strategy they use is to allow the vines to overproduce. Without limiting the yields of the vines by selectively cutting off a percentage of the grapes to enhance the growth, energy, and thus the character of the remaining grapes, the large corporate wineries have more juice of a lesser quality per vineyard acre with which to produce wine, whereas the smaller Spanish producer will take more pride in their final product and properly prune their vines. This Spanish Tierra de Castilla Albaliza Tempranillo and Garnacha blend has delicious fruit flavors."

"This is good. I'm planning a Cuban pulled pork dinner tonight. Would this wine go with the meal?" Jacob asked.

"It certainly would. It has enough fruit body to soften the spiciness of the pork. The last wine we're going to taste today is a red wine from Argentina, so fasten your seat belts for a trip back to the southern hemisphere. A discussion about red wines from Argentina usually centers around the Malbec grape varietal. The wine we're going to taste, however, is made from the Bonarda grape, the most widely planted in Argentina. Not much is shipped out of the country for processing elsewhere. This wine is richer, bigger, and more full bodied than the Albaliza Spanish wine we just tasted. It certainly has more weight, more depth with floral aromas and upfront fruit flavors. It is not heavy with tannins and goes down soft and easy. This Broquel Bonarda also goes well with spicy foods. I'd serve it with a good steak or pork sausage meal. What do you think?" I asked.

"I see what you mean. It is smooth and fresh," Jacob replied.

"I hope taking this wine tasting trip around the world took your mind off of those profit-loss spreadsheets for a few minutes."

"It certainly did. I can't thank you enough. Well, I better get back to the store. Give me a bottle of the Italian wine," Jacob decided.

"One Nino Franco Prosecco Rustico coming up!"

*P*arable *R*eflections

I held back on much more I wanted to share with Jacob about why I felt Pop More Corks was thriving even though my till wasn't always overflowing at the end of a working day, but hopefully Jacob would be in again and our conversation about what is really important in life, and in business, would continue.

Yes, it is ultimately about the bottom line, but running a successful business should mean much more to the business owner. Yes, it is always about what has to be done on a daily basis to make sure your business is running smoothly, but for all the right reasons.

Whereas a proprietor must be concerned about money, profit and loss should never be the main focus of your day.

The Apostle Mark penned the proverb, "What does it profit a man to gain the whole world and lose his soul."

In business, money is important, but it should not be the measure of success. Running a business, a product or service is offered to the public. Many hours during many long days, over months and years are spent operating the business. It is important that the core of your company represents something you are passionate about for all the right reasons.

Those right reasons involve your intention to serve your customers and in serving make a difference for good in their lives.

As the Pop More Corks clock reached 7:00 PM, once again it was time to close and lock the doors. Key in hand, I thought my evening mantra.

As I close this door, I am thankful for all the wonderful people and experiences that have been brought to me this day.

25

WHEN DO WE HAVE ENOUGH STUFF?

As I open this door, may I be open to allowing all possibilities to be brought to me. I ask to be receptive to whatever and whoever comes my way this glorious day.

"Dorothy, so good to see you again. What's new with you these days?" I inquired, welcoming a loyal Pop More Corks customer who'd been stopping in regularly.

"I want a special bottle of Ice wine to celebrate my boyfriend Larry's retirement, although I'm not sure it will turn out to be a celebration or a wake?" Dorothy opened.

"If I'm going to help you, I really need to know more . . . will it be a happy or sad occasion? It sounds like it will be a little of both. So, why is that?" I asked.

"Well, I've finally got a partner to share my retirement years. We'll be able to travel whenever we want and I'll be able to get him out to Tango more often! I suppose I should be happy about all that," Dorothy shared.

"How did that happen? I thought Larry loved teaching, at least, as I recall, he's been teaching for 30 some years, hasn't he?" I asked.

"Yes, that's true, but he came home the other day and said he'd just had enough of student insolence, and they don't treat each other any better. He said the money just wasn't worth the aggravation any more," Dorothy added, shaking her head.

"That couldn't have been an easy decision for him. A teacher should be able to walk into any classroom and have the cooperation of the class, but that's just not the way things are these days," I said.

"No, it wasn't easy for him, and we talked about what, if anything, he could do to start enjoying teaching again, but he's just had enough," she said.

"What did Larry think was at the heart of the problem?"

"Every year, the children have become harder and harder to manage. They seem to have little use for school and no sense of showing respect for authority in general or for the authority in the classroom, the teacher. We weren't raised that way. What's wrong with this generation?" Dorothy asked, genuinely frustrated and upset for her dear companion, Larry.

"They key seems to be what you said about how you were raised," I suggested.

"I know what you're getting at. These kids really aren't being raised the way we were. In most cases either both parents are working, or there is only one parent trying to manage the family. Who's going to be there to teach the students how to behave if the parents aren't available?" Dorothy declared.

"It seems to boil down to the fact that people feel the need to have so many material things," I suggested.

"You may be right, and if that's so, it explains what's happened to the family as we knew it. With both parents working to earn enough money for all those things, those cell phones, those expensive video game systems, those high priced designer clothes and shoes . . . the children end up with either absent parents or parents too tired to properly supervise what their children are doing," Dorothy added.

"That sounds about right. I know my parents were there to respond to a teacher who called to complain about my behavior in school and I always got in trouble worse at home than I did at school. Of course, my mother didn't work and someone was always home to get calls like that. Today's kids are raising themselves, and that's not good," I shared.

"Is there any turning this around?" Dorothy lamented.

"It's got to start with changing our cultural priorities. Families have to find a way to live with less so that they can free up more time and energy to get back to raising their children," I shared.

"Are you suggesting that we go back to the days when the man was the breadwinner and the wife stayed home?" Dorothy wondered, not at all comfortable with that misogynist position.

"Not at all. It doesn't matter who is available, the man or the woman, or both, through some sort of compromise at work, allowing one or both parents more time to participate in the important job of shaping our children's values," I suggested.

"Things certainly have become complicated in today's world, but in my personal life, things are about to get a whole lot less complicated. Now, how about suggesting a good Ice wine to, yes, *celebrate* Larry's retirement?" Dorothy asked, apparently relieved to have decided that it was all right for Larry to leave behind the troubles in today's classroom.

"I've got a nice Jackson-Triggs Ice wine from Canada that I think you'll love," I suggested.

"I've had and enjoyed Ice wine before, but refresh my memory about what makes it so unique?" Dorothy asked.

"You know, the grapes hang on the vine until very late in the growing season, get fully ripe, then, with luck, before the grapes pass their peak there is a freeze. Under just the right conditions, the water in the grapes becomes frozen, but there is more liquid inside the grape. This highly concentrated juice resists freezing because of its sugar content and is intensely flavored. While frozen, the grapes have this nectar separated from the frozen pulp during a squeezing and straining process. Only small amounts of this precious fluid is collected, processed, and fermented into Ice wine," I shared.

"Well, that explains the expense of the wine, but it is well worth every penny, especially as a way to mark a celebration!" Dorothy replied.

"Now, don't forget, you only serve a few ounces of this wine at a sitting. It is intensely sweet and rich and must be sipped to be enjoyed and appreciated," I added.

"I remember—we've been through this before as I recall."

"I just hope Larry can celebrate his retirement and not view his decision as some sore of failure on his part."

"I agree. He deserves to feel good about everything he's contributed over the years to so many of his students who did care and did try to benefit from his teaching."

*P*_{arable} *R*_{eflections}

Dorothy and I weren't about to solve such a fundamental social problem during one intense conversation, but we did identify an area that needs attention if an even more fundamental global problem is to be solved.

There are far too many human beings, too many children, who go to bed hungry night after night in a world with more than enough resources to go around, but those in control of world policies do not seem to care about their suffering.

This is a Karmic problem with global repercussions. Until all are safe, fed, clothed, sheltered, and educated, the resulting imbalance will continue to breed unrest, terrorism, war, and mistrust. We are all connected with strong interdependent bonds that we ignore at our own peril.

The seeds of hate that led to 9/11 were sown from the material imbalance that separates those with much, from those with little in our world.

Sharing is the obvious, but oh so politically difficult solution. It will take a great awakening throughout our collective consciousness to first recognize this problem, then, proceed to take the necessary political action to address it. At the heart of this change will be the recognition that those of us with much can still live good lives if we learn to live with less in order to share from our abundance with those less fortunate.

As the Pop More Corks clock reached 7:00 PM, once again it was time to close and lock the doors. Key in hand, I thought my evening mantra.

As I close this door, I am thankful for all the wonderful people and experiences that have been brought to me this day.

26

WHERE HAVE YOU BEEN?

As I open this door, may I be open to allowing all possibilities to be brought to me. I ask to be receptive to whatever and whoever comes my way this glorious day.

Angela and I have always been good personal friends, and at one time also closely connected on a spiritual level, but when circumstances put distance between us, although we both felt the inclination and still felt our spiritual bond, neither of us acted to reach out to rekindle what we once shared.

Then, one day I responded to an impulse to call, and Angela answered, very happy to hear from her old friend.

"David, I'm sorry so much time has passed, but I was thinking about you and just out of curiosity, I googled the name of your store, Pop More Corks, to see what I could find out about what's been going on in your life since we last saw each other, and to my surprise, your book came up. Congratulations! What's that all about?" Angela was pleased to say.

"You know, it's my small story. I've already shared most of basics with you about what I've been through, but the book has the details and some other things I wanted to pass on to people."

"David, you've got a great story and I'm glad you've taken this step to put it out there. It seems like things are going well for you."

"Yes, I have been fortunate. Why don't you come by sometime this weekend? It would be great to see you!" I suggested.

Angela followed through and stopped in that Sunday afternoon.

"How long have you been open, now?" Angela asked after giving me a big, long, warm hug.

"Just over a year and I can't complain. Every month business gets better, but more than that, each day I feel so good about where I am and what I'm doing."

"So, the sign out front mentions that wine tasting goes on here! I think I'd like some advice on just the right wine for a romantic dinner I'm planning for my boyfriend, and while suggesting, make sure they are wines you like as well. Then, I know they'll be good!" Angela said.

"I can do that."

"Can we start with a white wine?"

"Sure, first, let's try this wine from Spain," I suggested, while pouring a sample into a glass for Angela to taste.

"That is good. Tell me about it."

"It is a Marquis de Gelida Lel Cep Cava. Cava is the name of the region in northeastern Spain and in this case also describes the type of wine. As you can see, it is a sparkling wine. It is produced in the same fashion as a Champagne, but of course it can't be called a Champagne since it doesn't come from the Champagne district of France. With few negatives, one of the many positives is its outstanding quality-to-price ratio. Instead of costing $40 or more a bottle, it is a moderately priced $14 wine and as such is considered one of the best-value sparkling wines in the entire world. It is a crisp, clean, easy drinking, dry style of sparkling wine to go well with a party or celebration, or any occasion where you want to feel a little special." I explained.

"That was great, what's next?"

"This wine is from the region of France called Bordeaux, and a smaller sub district, Graves. As you can see, it is a white wine. When you are making white wine in that region of France, by law, if the name 'Graves' is on the label, only three types of grapes can be used. In this wine, the formula is for 75% Sauvignon Blanc, and 25% Semillion grapes. The third possible grape variety, Muscadelle, is not used in this particular wine. Because you're using two different grape varieties, each brings its unique characteristics to the blend. The Sauvignon Blanc adds a nice crisp herbaceous quality along with a distinct citrus character with grapefruit tones. The Semillion grape has a richer profile including fig and melon flavors. What's also exceptional about this wine is how it is produced. Many of us are used to Chardonnays fermented in oak barrels, adding barrel aging flavors to the wine. This Bordeaux from Graves is produced in stainless steel vats resulting in the pure crisp clean flavor of the grapes. This would be an outstanding wine to go with fish or scallops.

"Switching to a red, let's try this Spanish wine from Jumilla in the northwestern region of Spain. This is an area of higher elevation, so the soils are thinner and rocky. You don't get big, lush wines from the grapes grown in this area, but rather a lighter, more austere, layered profile. The first wine is Luzon Verde. It is made from only one grape variety,

Monastrell, and comes from a 100% organic vineyard. So we're dealing with organic Monastrell grapes from the Jumilla region of Spain, from a winery called Luzon. It has a floral aroma with an earthy character. It is an easy-drinking fruit-forward style of red wine. The next wine is from the south-central part of France.

"This Chateau Pesquie is from the Rhone River Valley area of France, and the Cotes de Ventoux sub district. In the Rhone you can blend up to twelve different grape varieties. This particular wine is made of two of them, Grenache and Syrah, and comes from vineyards that average over 50 years old. Such mature vines give the wine more intensity and character than those from younger vines. Grenache will always lend a certain white pepper spiciness to the wine while the Syrah adds a dark fruity backbone with body. This Chateau Pesquie would go with a meat dish like a braised lamb shank or a veal osso buco where during long, slow cooking the fat gets rendered out into a rich sauce. This is a wine that has the body and weight to stand up to that rich sauce. The next wine is a departure from the Old World wines we've tasted so far.

"This New World wine is from Australia. Generally speaking, Old World wines are more about linear layers of flavor, spiciness, and earthy tones, where the flavors distribute themselves first on the tip of the tongue, working to the back. New World wines, on the other hand, those from California, Chile, Australia, and New Zealand, are going to be much more about big, rich, mouth-filling, fruit-forward flavors where the flavors explode on the tongue from side to side. New World wines can sacrifice some complexity in order to achieve the intense burst of flavor experienced in the mouth. This next southern Australian wine, Pillar Box Red, is from Padthway, not too far from Adelaide.

"In this area, and compared to the typical Old World wine producing area, there is a warmer climate. As a result, the grapes ripen more thoroughly and contain more sugars which results, upon fermentation, with that more mouth-filling fruit-forward character. This wine is a blend of three grape varieties, Shiraz, Cabernet Sauvignon, and Merlot. Taste this wine and you'll find it to be soft, lush, smooth, and mouth filling with few tannins. It comes across as being juicy and fruit forward, yet with enough weight and body. I would serve this Pillar Box Red with spicy foods like a blackened strip steak or sautéed Cajun chicken breast. The fruit-forward character of the wine will soften the spiciness of the food. What you don't want with such meals are wines with a dry, bitter, tannic edge where the tannins will end up competing with the spices."

"David, you mentioned two similar sounding grape varieties, the Syrah grape in one of the earlier wines, and Shiraz in the Pillar Box Red. They sound so similar by name. Are they the same grape or are they different?" Angela questioned.

"My compliments on picking that up. In fact, they are the same grape, but there's more to the story. The grape variety began in the Middle East, in Iran. From there it was brought to France where it became famous in the Rhone region where it was spelled Syrah. For years it was one of the main grapes used in wines like Cotes du Ventoux, Cotes du Rhone, and Chateauneuf-du-Pape. From France, the grape was brought to Australia along with a wave of immigration. These new Australians from France brought many of their foods and traditions with them. When they planted that Syrah grape, being the rebellious Aussies that they were, they renamed the Syrah grape to Shiraz. Now, whereas the two represent the same grape variety, the style of a grape grown in France will differ from one grown in Australia.

"The French Syrah grape will tend to be much more layered, herbaceous, earthy, and comes across as being dryer, expressing the terroir and also much less about the fruit, whereas the Shiraz from Australia presents a big, juicy, jammy, mouth-filling taste experience in wines where it is used. So, watch for the spelling on a wine label. If the producer knows what they're doing, you can expect the wine with those grapes to display the characteristics of the region where it was grown. Now, let's go back to a white wine. I've saved this for last because it has some residual sweetness to it. Usually, when tasting wines, you'd taste whites before reds and from lighter to more full-bodied. You always taste from drier to sweeter. Even though this is a white wine, because it is sweeter we've saved it for last."

"Sip this and tell me what you think it tastes like," I began, knowing where my suggestion would lead.

"Peaches, I definitely taste peaches!" Angela replied, surprised at how easy it was to discern the delicate bouquet.

"You're absolutely right! That was a St. Suprey Moscato from California, and like every other wine in my store, it is made entirely from grapes."

"How can that be, the flavor is so obvious?"

"It's all about the magic of the fermentation process. Since it's a white wine, the skins are cast aside prior to fermentation. The sugars in the juice become food for the special yeasts chosen by producers to ferment the wine. During the process, depending on the type of yeast and the temperature, the sugars are transformed into aromatic molecules with recognizable fruit-forward flavors, in the case of Moscato grapes, peaches. Of course, depending on where the grapes are grown, each type of grape has a unique set of raw materials for the fermentation process to transform.

I'm making it sound straight forward, but the process is only controllable to a certain extent which is why an outstanding bottle of wine is as much about magic and art as it is about the grapes and the soil and the barrels. So, when you pick up a glass of Cabernet Sauvignon and taste black current and black cherry and blackberry, the same fermentation magic is responsible," I explained.

"That's amazing. How would it best be used with a dinner?" Angela asked.

"It's for after dinner or served either with or instead of a desert. It has some residual sugar and sweetness, yet it's still light and refreshing."

"That's a lot to take in, but it does help me understand my reaction to each wine we tasted. I'm most impressed with the peachy St. Suprey Moscato. Wrap a bottle up for me," Angela said.

"Good choice!"

"So, tell me more about the book, how it came together, and what you think it's going to mean to your life?" Angela asked of her dear old friend and soul mate who she could tell was at a crossroads of an important life passage.

"No matter what happens with the book, my store, Pop More Corks, will always be an important part of life. Through my daily interactions with customers, I'm privileged to not only share my knowledge about wines, but more importantly, I'm also able to share my life experiences, values, beliefs, and insights, many of which came while recovering from my stroke, through often deep conversations that develop during what begins as a casual wine tasting.

"Although I will always value what goes on here at the store, I know that through the book I'll have a chance to share ideas and experiences with a wider audience. It's a great opportunity that's been handed to me and I need to find a way to explore developing the book's potential as a way to get a message out there.

"And so, I'll be spending time refining the book, finding a publisher, getting the book to the public, and making room in my schedule to promote the book and in doing so, sharing the good things I've been experiencing."

"That's a lot to put on your plate. Why does this mean so much to you?" Angela couldn't help but ask realizing just how demanding it would be for anyone, much less someone in my condition, to test his limits.

"Just take today. There were people in the store who were back for second, third, and fourth visits. For others, it was their first visit—many indicating someone suggested they stop in. At first I didn't realize why I felt so good at the end of the day, but it didn't take long to realize that sharing information about wine almost always led to sharing important ideas, like the important role of diversity and staying connected to nature, the source of our existence. When I open up about deeper subjects, my guests seem to do the same and all involved benefit from the experience of sharing during an open, honest conversation. I can sense their appreciation. They leave Pop More Corks feeling good about more than merely having a special bottle of wine to take home."

"I think I understand now why you're writing the book. I wish I had more of what you're feeling in my life right now," Angela replied.

"I'm not special. Anyone can get to a place where they're responding to a calling, a sense they were meant to do something—that you're following the best possible path for your life. You know you're on that path when you feel an exhilarating creative passion for what you're doing. Getting there is not always easy and not without risks, but the benefits are almost always worth the risks."

"I'll try to remember that," Angela said before leaving.

*P*arable *R*eflections

The mystery of Synchronicity was once again at work. Two souls, once close, had lost touch, but ongoing thoughts, one for the other, began to stir the caldron of Synchronous soup and eventually triggered a renewed opportunity to share and grow close again.

Whether our soul mate relationship revs up again remains to be seen, but Angela's encouragement to share my story in print was just what I needed to hear that day.

When you reach out to help someone, you inevitably help yourself, and the world.

As the Pop More Corks clock reached 7:00 PM, once again it was time to close and lock the doors. Key in hand, I thought my evening mantra.

As I close this door, I am thankful for all the wonderful people and experiences that have been brought to me this day.

GLOSSARY

ICE WINE

The grapes used to produce Ice Wine hang on the vine until very late in the growing season, get fully ripe, then, with luck, before the grapes pass their peak, there is a freeze. Under just the right conditions, the water in the grapes becomes frozen, but there is more liquid inside the grape. This highly concentrated juice resists freezing because of its sugar content and is intensely flavored. While frozen, the grapes have this nectar separated from the frozen pulp during a squeezing and straining process. Only small amounts of this precious fluid is collected, processed, and fermented into Ice Wine. You only serve a few ounces of this wine at a sitting. It is intensely sweet and rich and must be sipped to be enjoyed and appreciated.

WINE & SULFITES

It is impossible for a wine not to have sulfites. Even organic wines have them. To make wine, grape juice is fermented. In that process, yeast converts sugar into alcohol, carbon dioxide, and among many other products, sulfites are generated. Organic wines do not have any extra added sulfites to extend their shelf life, as is often the policy of many of the larger wineries.

At times you will and at times you won't see the word "sulfites" on the label. Some labels will say, "Contains Added Sulfites" and those will be wines from mass produced corporate wineries. Because they are producing hundreds of thousands of cases, they add sulfites to keep the wine stable over long periods of time. Other labels will say, "Contains Sulfites" which means that the levels of sulfites have reached the point where by law they have to be listed on the label. When you find a wine where sulfites are not listed anywhere on the label, that simply means that the sulfite level is below that legal standard.

APPENDIX

WINE – QUESTIONS & ANSWERS

Question #1

As a consumer, wines can be very confusing. With so many different wines to choose from, how do you make the right choice without experiencing how it tastes?

Start by exploring what kind of grape appeals to you. Then, think about where you would like that grape to be grown. At that point, you'll find yourself with a much more manageable group of wines to choose from. What you can be confident of is that a group of wines of a particular type from a particular region will taste much more alike than that type from another part of the world.

When deciding within a region, the producer is not as important as the characteristics of the grapes from that region used by those producers.

Question #2

I just bought a bottle of expensive wine and when I got home noticed it had a twist off top. Should I take it back?

Twist-off tops are perfectly good ways to seal in the freshness, or seal out the external environment, and have no bearing on the quality of the wine inside. There are outstanding $100 bottles of wine produced with twist-off tops.

Question #3

The holidays are coming up. What would be the perfect wine to go with turkey?

For a gathering like Thanksgiving or Christmas, the "perfect" wine has less to do with the food being served and more to do with whether most of your guests will enjoy the wine you select.

As far as a wine recommendation to specifically go with turkey, a nice Gewurtzraminer from the Alsace region in France has enough flavor to stand up to the rich taste of turkey, but with a touch a fruit to make the average wine drinker happy along with enough interest and floral aromas and spice, to please a wine connoisseur. Another recommendation would be a light style Pinot Noir.

Question #4

How would you distinguish between the character and style of a wine?

A wine can have a certain character that represents a style. A Cabernet Sauvignon from Paso Robles in California is going to have a certain character that derived from its origin. It would be big, rich, fruit forward, with a little bit of a dry, earthy flavor. Although its character will represent the place it comes from, in a broader, more general sense, stylistically it will be easily recognized as New World.

Old World wines are from Europe, predominantly from France, Italy, Portugal, and Spain, while New World wines originate from Australia, New Zealand, Argentina, the United States, and Chile.

Old World wines are about layers of flavor. When you smell the wine you get that they are substantially more aromatic. They will present one distinct flavor on the tip of your tongue, another in the middle, and others on the back of your tongue. The flavor profile is linear—front to back in the mouth.

New World wines are about big, upfront flavors that showcase in a bold way the intense fruit flavors that fill the mouth up from side to side without the more subtle distinctions.

To classify a wine, then, stylistically begin with Old or New World, then, their character will take you to the specific region where the grapes were grown and the wine was produced.

Question #5

Where do the distinct flavors and aromas of other fruits come from in wine?

Wine begins as grape juice which contains a lot of sugar. A yeast culture is introduced that begins to consume the sugar as a food source. During the process, the sugar is converted into drinkable ethyl alcohol and carbon dioxide. Sugar is a six-carbon chain molecule known as a carbohydrate, a combination of carbon and water molecules. So far, this sounds scientific, but during the process of fermentation, the yeast reformulates the sugar molecule.

There is a wine on the Pop More Corks shelves that customers swear smells and tastes of peaches and apricots. They are correct, it does, and yet there are no wines on the shelves blended with any other juice than from grapes. The yeast is capable of creating more than alcohol from its sugar food source. It is able, through a complex biochemical process, to create subtle and distinct new flavors, such as those naturally occurring in peaches and apricots.

That is the magic of what goes on inside a bottle of fine wine. It is only understood in general terms and only marginally controlled through the selection of yeast and monitoring the temperature, but the end result is a gift to the wine and to mankind.

If a wine does not go through that process, it can not develop the character palette of unique flavors. When the alcohol is removed from a wine, much of that magic, that complexity, is also removed.

For example, some of the unique characteristics of a wine comes from the grape itself, such as a Cabernet Sauvingon grape, and some of the style of the wine comes from where the grape is grown, such as from the Paso Robles region in California. The climate there is hot, dusty, and dry. The grapes from there tend to ripen fully and produce a big, rich, fat, juicy flavor. With those factors in place, the yeast goes to work recreating a unique flavor profile.

Question #6

Are the Syrah and Shiraz grape varieties the same?

In fact, they are the same grape, but there's more to the story. The grape variety began in the Middle East, in Iran. From there it was brought to France where it became famous in the Rhone region where it was spelled Syrah. For years it was one of the main grapes used in wines like Cotes du Ventoux, Cotes du Rhone, and Chateauneuf-du-Pape. From France, the grape was brought to Australia with a wave of immigration. These new Australians from France brought many of their foods and traditions with them. When they planted that Syrah grape, being the rebellious Aussies that they were, they renamed the Syrah grape to Shiraz. Now, whereas the two represent the same grape variety, the style of a grape variety grown in France will differ from one grown in Australia.

The French Syrah grape will tend to be much more layered, herbaceous, and earthy and comes across as being dryer, expressing the terroir and much less about the fruit whereas the Shiraz from Australia presents a big, juicy, jammy, mouth-filling taste experience in wines where it is used. So, watch for the spelling on a wine label. If the producer knows what they're doing, you can expect the wine with those grapes to display the characteristics of the region where it was grown.

WINE TASTINGS

PP. 53-60

Preston Sauvignon Blanc, Dry Creek Valley, Sonoma County

Gazela Vinho Verde, Portugal

Chateaux Barrail Chevrol, Fronsac, France

Barco Reale di Carmingano, Toscana, Italy

Piesporter Michelsberg Riesling Spatlese, Germany

PP. 80-84

Sartori Pinot Grigio, Veneto, Italy

Gaierhof Pinot Grigio, Trentino Alto Adige, Italy

Ponzi Pinot Gris, Willamette Valley, Oregon

Monte Volpe Pinot Grigio, Mendocino, California

P. 152

Hugel Gentil, Alsace, France

PP. 155-161

Jean Garaudet Hautes-Cotes de Beaune, Burgundy, France (Pinot Noir)

Te Kairanga Pinot Noir, Marlborough, New Zealand

Ponzi Willamette Valley Pinot Noir, Oregon

Santa Barbara Winery Pinot Noir, Santa Rita Hills, Santa Barbara, California

PP. 167-172

Les Douze Fitou, Languedoc, France

Luzon de Luzon, Jumilla, Spain

Poitevin, Medoc, France, Cabernet Sauvignon Blend

Nugan Cabernet Sauvignon, Southeastern Australia

P. 174-179

Marquis de Gelida el Cep Cava, Spain

Chateaux du Fort Roquetaillade, Graves Blanc, France

Luzon Verde, Jumilla, Spain

Chateau Pesquie, Cotes de Ventoux, France

Pillar Box Red, Southeast Australia

PP. 179-184

Nino Franco Prosecco Rustico, Veneto, Italy

Ken Forester Petite Chenin Blanc, Stellenbosch, South Africa

Buehler Chardonnay, Russian River Valley, Sonoma, California

Albaliza, Tierra de Castilla, Spain

BIBLIOGRAPHY

The Power of Myth, Joseph Campbell, Anchor, 1991

The Power of Myth (CD Set), Joseph Campbell, Highbridge Audio, 2001

Hero with a Thousand Faces, Joseph Campbell, Princeton University Press, 19972

Creative Visualization, Shakti Gawain, Full Circle Publishing, 2003

Parabola, Summer 2003

NOTE FROM THE AUTHOR

There are any number of reasons why you, the reader, may have been drawn to *Pop More Corks*. Perhaps you have always been interested in learning more about wine and the global wine culture. It may be that you've struggled to rebuild your life after a personal tragedy or an interest in broad spiritual concepts. In any case, I hope my story to move forward after a stroke has given you hope and direction.

I'm open to any further discussion on the subject.

To reach out to me personally, please email: dbiegemann@earthlink.net

David Biegemann